AIRLIN

McDonnell Douglas MD-80

ARTHUR PEARCY

Acknowledgements

The Author wishes to thank the many airlines who supplied photographs, and special thanks to Harry Gann, Manager, Aircraft Information with the Douglas Aircraft Company at Long Beach, California who devoted many hours sorting out many of the transparencies used in this book.

First published in the UK in 1993
by Airlife Publishing Ltd.

British Library Cataloguing in Publication Data
A catalogue record for this book
is available from the British Library

ISBN 1 85310 358 6

Printed in Singapore by Kyodo Printing Co. (S'pore Pte Ltd.)

Airlife Publishing Ltd.

101 Longden Road, Shrewsbury SY3 9EB, England.

Introduction

Late in the 1970s the Douglas Aircraft Company located at Long Beach, California, commenced studies to further enhance the performance and capabilities of their successful DC-9 airliner. Five major versions of the twin, high-T tail DC-9 had been developed, commencing with the Series 10 which first flew on 25 February 1965. This led to the Series 20, 30, 40 and 50. In all 976 DC-9 airliners were delivered and some 284 operators, including military air arms, used the type. Today over 900 are still in service.

The new aircraft was initially designated DC-9 Series 55, however, in August 1977, that designation was changed to DC-9 Super 80. That series first flew on 18 October 1979, the aircraft being N980DC c/n 48000 f/n 909. In line with the company's policy to incorporate the McDonnell Douglas name in all commercial aircraft built by the Corporation, the new version was redesignated the MD-80 Series in July 1983. At the present time, the MD-80 is being delivered in sub-versions as the MD-81, -82, -83, -87 and the -88, differing in specific customer requirements in power plant, size and avionics.

With a tradition dating back to 1934 of stretching the fuselage of its Douglas Commercial airliners, the McDonnell Douglas Corporation subsidiary, the Douglas Aircraft Company, had become by the mid-seventies the almost undisputed champion of capacity increase mainly through lengthening the fuselage. To all intents and purposes the MD-80 airliner was not a new aircraft.

The DC-9 Super 80 with JT8D-209 re-fanned engines and other new features was launched in October 1977, following strong pressure from Swissair. Earlier in 1977 MDC had insisted it was only an order from a major US carrier that would persuade the go-ahead. The launch orders included 15 firm and five options from Swissair, eight firm and four options from Austrian Airlines, as well as a conditional commitment for four aircraft from the US regional carrier, Southern Airways. In June 1978 Southern cancelled the order, a blow to MDC, but this was soon offset when Pacific Southwest Airlines decided to adopt the type as a replacement for its Boeing 727s.

On 5 October 1980, Swissair commenced DC-9-81 service on its Zurich to London route, whilst in the USA Pacific Southwest Airlines (PSA) became the first US carrier to fly Series 80 airliners when it inaugurated services in California from its San Diego base on 16 December 1980. The DC-9-82 (MD-82) entered service with Republic Airlines in August 1981, the MD-83 with Finnair in July 1985, the MD-87 with Austrian Airlines and Finnair during November 1987, and finally the MD-88 with Delta Air Lines of Atlanta, Georgia, in January 1988.

The MD-80, like earlier DC-9 models, was certificated for two pilot operation. However, the Airline Pilots Association (ALPA) strenuously opposed the two-pilot crewing arrangement, attempting to impose a three-pilot crew on US carriers. As a result of the position, Southern Airways cancelled its order whilst other long-term customers, notably Delta and Eastern, were initially unable to order MD-80 series airliners as they could ill-afford to comply with the ALPA demand. So it was PSA who became the first airline to fly the MD-80 in the USA, as its non-union crews were prepared to fly the airliners with just two pilots as certificated. Had the ALPA restriction remained unchallenged, the future of other MD-80 sales would surely have been in jeopardy. Fortunately, a Presidential task force ruled as far back as 1981, that a third crew member was not required for safety purposes.

This opened the way ahead for large scale orders for the new airliner. American Airlines took advantage, in October 1982, of the unique marketing offer by MDC to lease its first 20 MD-82s for an initial two-year period. American initially purchased 67 MD-82s and optionised 100 more in February 1984. As of 30 November 1992, American had 260 MD-80s in service, the largest fleet of any single type of aircraft outside Russia – with many more MD-80s either on order or option. The largest non-US customers as of 30 November 1992, were the Scandinavian Airlines System (SAS) with 57 MD-80s in service and more on order, followed by Alitalia with 32 MD-80s with a further 38 operated by its domestic ATI and lots more on order. Japan Air System operates 28 MD-80s with more on order plus options.

Long Beach delivered 140 MD-80s in 1991, one over the record of 139 in 1990. Since the MD-80 programme was initiated in 1980, MDC has delivered 1036, the airliner being operated by more than 50 customers around the world. Combined with the DC-9, the intermediate range twin-jet programme has now produced and put into service 2,012 aircraft by the end of 1992, making it one of the most successful jet programmes in aviation history. The order book contains not only firm commitments, but options and reserves.

MCDONNELL DOUGLAS MD-80 SPECIFICATIONS					
	MD-81	MD-82	MD-83	MD-87	MD-88
First flight	18 Oct 1979	8 Jan 1981	17 Dec 1984	4 Dec 1986	15 Aug 1987
Wing span ft/in metres.	107 10 32.87	107 10 32.87	107 10 32.87	107 10 32.87	107 10 32.87
Length ft/in metres	147 10 45.06	147 10 45.06	147 10 45.06	119 1 36.30	147 10 45.06
Height ft/in metres	29 8 9.04	29 8 9.04	29 8 9.04	30 6 9.30	29 8 9.04
Wing area sq/ft sq/metres.	1,209 112.3	1,209 112.3	1,209 112.3	1,209 112.3	1,209 112.3
Max t/o weight lbs. k/g.	140,000 63,503	149,500 67,812	160,000 72,575	140,000 63,503	160,000 72,575
Max cruise speed mph km/hr	575 925	575 925	575 925	575 925	575 925
Max range miles /km	1,590 2,565	2,140 3,445	2,725 4,387	2,140 3,445	1,800 2,880
Service ceiling ft./ metres	37,000 11,200	37,000 11,200	37,000 11,200	37,000 11,200	37,000 11,200
Engines (two) Pratt & Whitney Thrust lb.	JT8D-209 18,500	JT8D-217 20,000	JT8D-209 JT8D-217/A JT8D-217C JT8D-219 21,000	JT8D-219 20,000	JT8D-219 21,000
First delivery customer/date.	Swissair 13 Sep 1980	Republic 5 Aug 1981	Finnair 19 Oct 1985	Transwede 4 Aug 1987	Delta 29 Dec 1987

ADRIA AIRWAYS (JP/ADR)   Jugoslavia

Adria Airways was formed in 1961, being reorganised in 1968 as part of the Interexport group, when the name was changed to Inex Adria Airways. In May 1986 the name was changed back to Adria Airways when it became an independent operator. It operates charter and scheduled services between Jugoslavia, Europe, the Middle East and North Africa. Scheduled domestic services link all the major cities in Jugoslavia. Additional seasonal domestic services are also operated between major cities in Jugoslavia and the holiday resorts on the Adriatic coast. International scheduled services are operated to Larnaca, Munich, London, Paris, Bari, Tel Aviv, Athens, Vienna, Frankfurt and Moscow.

The McDonnell Douglas aircraft inventory for 31 March 1992 lists Adria as having three DC-9s and five MD-80s. In August 1978 Adria placed an order for one MD-81 and two MD-82s, these entering service in 1981. In addition to the services already mentioned the MDC airliners are also used on package tour flights and contract charters carrying migrant workers between Jugoslavia and West Germany.

Adria had its licence to fly returned on 16 January 1992,

following its removal on 25 October 1991, by the Federal secretariat of Transport & Communications, caused by the war between the Croats and Serbs in Jugoslavia from June 1991. With effect from 26 December 1991 a new registration came into being which applied to all of the Adria fleet. The MD-82 YU-ANO became SL-ABO registered in the independent Republic of Slovenia. YU-ANO was one of the two Adria airliners leased to Croatia Airlines.

Early in 1992 the Adria Airlines livery was given a completely new design involving an overall white aircraft, with a large styled 'ADRIA' title covering the front of the fuselage in large dark blue letters. A heart shape design in turquoise and dark blue covers the tail unit whilst a small Jugoslav national flag is painted on the leading edge of the fin near the fuselage. The registration is in dark blue on the fuselage adjacent to the engine nacelles, these having 'MD-82' in turquoise. Depicted is MD-82 YU-ANC c/n 48087 f/n 1035 which was delivered to Inex Adria on 2 April 1982, and seen in the new attractive livery. *(Chris Doggett)*

AEROMEXICO (AM/AMX)

Mexico

Established on 14 September 1934 Aeronaves de Mexico, became Aeromexico in February 1972. Its first route was between Mexico City and Acapulco in the same month that the airline was formed. In Mexico more companies have existed than in any other Latin American country throughout its airline history. Subsequently since 1952 Aeronaves de Mexico absorbed several smaller airlines in Mexico, including Lamsa, Aerovias, Reforma, Aerolineas Mexicanas SA and Guest Aerovios. In 1952 the airline was nationalised and the Pan American holding passed to the Mexican Government. During 1970, under a general plan, the domestic airlines of Mexico were rationalised into an integrated air-transport system under the control of Aeronaves de Mexico and organised into eight smaller carriers.

In April 1988 the airline was declared bankrupt by the Mexican Government's owners. For some years the airline had been over-staffed, and an attempt the same year to reduce costs led to a major strike which grounded the company. A liquidator was appointed and took control of the airline's operations, drawing up a six-month recovery plan in preparation for privatisation. Despite an overall cut-back services were restarted to 30 domestic destinations and five cities in the United States. A 65 per cent controlling share in the airline was acquired in November 1988 by Gruppo Dictum, a consortium of Mexican business interests. The Mexican pilots' union, ASPA, purchased the remaining shares.

The latest Aeromexico livery, introduced in the early 1980s, is striking and consists of a highly-polished natural metal finish, this acting as a perfect backdrop for the bright orange cheatline which on the MD-80s is broad and takes in the windowline. A white Mexican birdman motif appears on the red tail unit. The Mexican national flag is just aft of the cockpit, whilst 'Aeromexico' in white appears on the cheatline. The engine nacelles are red-orange and the aircraft registration appears in white at the rear of the fuselage. It is not unusual for airlines to adopt a highly-polished natural metal finish, as this pays dividends by saving a considerable amount of weight, and subsequently is a fuel saver. Depicted is MD-82 XA-AMJ c/n 48068 f/n 1031 on a pre-delivery test flight carrying the temporary registration N1003Y. It was delivered to Aeromexico on 22 December 1981. (MDC)

AEROCANCUN (IAE/ACU/X7C)   Mexico

Aerocancun Aeronautica de Cancun is a new Mexican charter carrier formed in 1989. By March 1990 it had ordered four A310 Airbus airliners for delivery between November 1991 and May 1993. With these new airliners flights are planned from the tourist resort of Cancun to points in the United States which include Bangor, Maine; Columbus, Ohio; New York, Philadelphia, Oakland, Washington DC., Denver, Detroit, Cincinnati, Baltimore, Chicago and Los Angeles. Cancun to Frankfurt, Germany, is also served plus major cities in Canada, plus Buenos Aires, Sao Paulo, Saint Maarten and other points in South America.

The McDonnell Douglas aircraft inventory for 31 March 1992 lists Aerocancun as having four MD-83 twin-jet airliners, these being on lease from the Guinness Peat Aviation Group (GPA).

These include VR-BMH c/n 49628 f/n 1582 ex EC-EOM of Oasis International, VR-BMI c/n 49629 f/n 1583 ex EC-EOY also of Oasis, and VR-BMJ c/n 49791 f/n 1644 ex F-ODTN.

An off-white fuselage finish with an emerald green tail unit is the highlight of the Aerocancun livery. The airline motif, three white curled images, appears on the tail unit. These are repeated forward of the title 'AEROCANCUN' in black on the forward fuselage top. The engine nacelles are white, and the registration placed on the rear fuselage above the last four windows, forward of the passenger door. Depicted is MD-83 VR-BMH which was delivered to Oasis International as EC-EOM on 25 April 1989 prior to lease by GPA to Aerocancun. *(MAP)*

AERO LLOYD (LL/AEF/XLL)   Germany

Aero Lloyd (Flugreisen Luftverkehrs KG) was founded on 5 December 1980 and commenced flying operations in March 1981, initially with a small fleet of three French Caravelle airliners. In May 1982, the first Douglas DC-9-32 was acquired by this Frankfurt based airline and since then the fleet has been considerably increased. The McDonnell Douglas aircraft inventory dated 30 November 1992 lists Aero Lloyd as operating three DC-9s and seventeen MD-80 twin-jet airliners.

Scheduled services were put into effect on 31 October 1988. Today Aero Lloyd operates passenger charter flights from its home base at Frankfurt to Dusseldorf, Hamburg, Munich, Hannover and Stuttgart to popular holiday resorts located in the Mediterranean and Canary Islands, and the Middle East. In addition the airline operates scheduled domestic services from Frankfurt to Hamburg and Munich, and from Hamburg to Dusseldorf. The airline has aimed, with some success, to undercut the air fares charged by Lufthansa.

On 1 December 1989 a Munich to Gatwick, London, service was inaugurated. Major shareholders are Air Charter Market, Dipl KimRein hold Braumer & Jan Kilmitz. The first MD-83 fitted out with 167-seats entered service in May 1986, this being followed by 137-seat MD-87s in the summer of 1988. The fleet of three DC-9-32s is supported by thirteen MD-83s and four MD-87s.

Livery of Aero Lloyd consists of a three colour – gold/orange/red fuselage band positioned below the windowline, extending from nose to tail. This is broken by the title 'AERO LLOYD' in black on the forward fuselage which is white to wing level then natural metal below. The white tail unit is decorated with the three colours of gold/orange/red, angled at 45 degrees with the airline title 'AERO LLOYD' in black. A small German national flag appears near the top of the tail unit. The engine nacelles are white decorated by the three-colour cheatline, and the registration is positioned over the last windows on the rear fuselage. McDonnell Douglas MD-83 D-ALLD c/n 49402 f/n 1261 delivered to Aero Lloyd on 25 March 1986 has been on lease to ZAS Airline of Egypt. Depicted is MD-83 D-ALLE c/n 49449 f/n 1354 delivered on 28 March 1987. *(MAP)*

AIR CALIFORNIA/
AIR CAL (ZCA/CO)

United States of America

It was during April 1981 that Air California became re-titled Air Cal, having initially commenced operations in January 1967. Its base was Orange County Airport, today known as John Wayne, in southern California. Following the collapse of its owner, Westgate California Corporation, the airline was placed under trusteeship from 1972 to 1981. Air Cal became 70 per cent owned by Aircal Investment. High frequency interstate one-class scheduled passenger services were operated between John Wayne Airport, Santa Ana, to Seattle/Tacoma; San Jose; San Francisco; Oakland; Portland; Sacramento' Reno/Lake Tahoe; Burbank and Los Angeles. Charter flights were authorised to other points in the United States.

Formed in April 1966, Air California placed two ex Continental Douglas DC-9s into service on its Santa Ana to San Francisco route. This was implemented after a long environmental battle against strong public objections to operating jet airliners out of the then small airport in Orange County which was surrounded by huge residential development. The next service with the DC-9 to

be added to the growing schedule, was San Jose to Oakland, all part of the process of developing high-frequency intra-state services.

The bright livery of Air Cal reflected the warm sunshine of California, the airliners having an overall white finish with a four colour cheatline made up of yellow and orange on the forward fuselage windowline, with lower colours of red and black, these being broader. At the fourteenth window the four colour cheatline stepped up with the red now on the windowline. Half of the tail unit was also decorated with the four aforementioned colours. The title 'AIRCAL' was on the top of the forward fuselage aft of the cockpit in black, repeated on the tail unit on the forward white portion in black and at an angle. Depicted is MD-82 N477AC c/n 48062 f/n 1015 delivered to Air Cal on 15 October 1981, and today this airliner is contained in the huge American Airlines fleet of MD-80s and still registered N477AC. It is seen on a pre-delivery test flight from Long Beach over the Pacific Ocean just off-shore. (MDC)

AIR LIBERTE (BT/LIB/ZLI)   France

Air Liberte is a fairly recently formed French charter carrier, founded in July 1987 and commencing operations with McDonnell Douglas twin-jet airliners in April 1988, with a single MD-83 F-GHED c/n 49576 f/n 1422, leased from the Irish based Guinness Peat Aviation Group. From its home base at Orly airport, near Paris, the airline operates passenger services to both European and Mediterranean holiday resorts and has introduced routes from Paris to Montreal and New York with its fleet of larger A.300 and A.310 Airbus airliners of which it has three. It has six MD-83s of which a number are leased, an example being F-GHEB c/n 49822 f/n 1539 leased in 1991 for a period to Minerve-Compagne Francaise de Transports Aeriens, having the Minerve titles in red under the Air Liberte fuselage and tail titles.

The 169-seat airliners in the MD-83 class are operated in an inclusive tour (IT) charter configuration from Paris, Lyons, Lille, Nantes and Basle in Switzerland, to the highly popular holiday resorts and destinations located in Greece, Jugoslavia, Israel, Egypt, Italy, Malta, Tunisia plus other locations in North Africa. One MD-83 is based at Monastir, flying from Air Liberte Tunisie. According to the McDonnell Douglas aircraft inventory dated 30 November 1992, this airline operates two MD-83s. The current fleet was delivered in time for the 1991 summer holiday season, some being delivered from Long Beach, others bought or leased from the second hand market.

The colourful and attractive livery includes the 'Air Liberte' titling in dark blue on the upper white fuselage and across the tail unit, whilst a red, white and dark blue sash sweeps up from the aircraft's nosewheel bay, narrowing and terminating at the title. It reappears again behind the titling to curve over the top of the rear fuselage. A similar design runs the height of the tail unit, again revolving around the titling, as on the fuselage, the title being positioned half-way up the fin. Depicted is F-GHHO c/n 49885 f/n 1689 seen during 1991. *(MAP)*

AIRSUR

Spain

AirSur was founded originally in 1985 as Canafrica Transportes Aereos and commenced charter operations in May 1986. The present AirSur title was adopted in June 1988.

The airline undertakes charter flights with two McDonnell Douglas MD-83 twin-jet airliners, obtained on lease from the Guinness Peat Aviation Group (GPA) based at Shannon airport, Eire, and delivered in May 1987. The 165-passenger aircraft provided inclusive tour (IT) services to Portugal, the mainland of Spain, and the holiday resorts in the Balearic and Canary Islands from points located in Austria, France, Germany, Italy, Ireland, the United Kingdom, north and west Africa, plus others. Early in 1992 AirSur commenced a Saturday charter service from Las Palmas, Hamburg, Palma, Majorca and return. The two MD-83 airliners are maintained by Swissair at Zurich airport, Switzerland.

AirSur livery includes an overall white finish, with dark blue cheatline below the windowline, from the first four passenger windows. This has a broad slant. The title 'AIRSUR' is on the top of the forward fuselage with a small Spanish national flag positioned behind. The tail design is not unlike a dolphin with three blue streaks. The registration is on the tail unit placed very high, and the engine nacelles are white with 'MD-83' in dark blue.

The two MD-83 airliners are EC-ECN c/n 49401 f/n 1357 which was ex EC-714 and EI-CBN, delivered on 29 April 1987, whilst the second, EC-ECO c/n 49442 f/n 1358 was delivered on 28 April 1987, and is depicted during 1991. *(MAP)*

AIRTOURS INTERNATIONAL (VZ/AAH/ZDG)

United Kingdom

Airtours International was formed in 1990, and is now an established successful United Kingdom charter carrier. The company commenced operations on 20 March 1991 with a fleet of five McDonnell Douglas MD-83 twin-jet airliners leased from Irish Aerospace Limited. The 167-seat airliners operate on both short and long-haul flights and for the first season three aircraft were based at Manchester, and one each at Birmingham and London Stansted, with operations from Cardiff, East Midlands, London Gatwick, Glasgow, Liverpool and Newcastle. With effect from November 1991, the London Stansted MD-83 was transferred to London Gatwick where the company plans increased business.

Three additional MD-83s were leased for the 1992 season as part of the company planned expansion, with one of the additional aircraft being based at East Midlands. Destinations served from the United Kingdom include Cyprus, Greece, Madeira, Malta, Spain, the Algarve, Tunisia and Turkey. There are also flights to Paris, France. Airline personnel number 300, and the company ICAO radio call-sign is 'Kestrel.'

The airline is a subsidiary of Airtours, one of the largest tour operators in the United Kingdom, which also owns Eurosites, a self-drive holiday company. Long-haul routes are planned for the future by Airtours International, to include the Bahamas, Barbados, Cancun, the Dominican Republic, Florida, Jamaica and Kenya. On 30 March 1991, the airline operated its first Newcastle to Palma, Majora, flight utilising MD-83 G-DAC c/n 49935 f/n 1773.

The airline's livery is based on an overall white fuselage with dark blue undersurface. At wing level a narrow emerald green pinstripe runs the length of the aircraft, this extending up the front of the dark blue tail unit in three staggered lines. The airlines 'A' emblem is styled on an emerald green globe design. The 'Airtours' title is styled under the windowline forward on the fuselage, whilst the rear portion of the MD-83 is dark blue, the engine nacelles being white. Depicted is N30016 c/n 49940 f/n 1788 which became G-TTPT seen on a pre-delivery test flight from Long Beach. *(Airtours)*

ALASKA AIRLINES (AS/ASA)

United States of America

Founded in 1932 as McGee Airways, Alaska Airlines adopted its present title during 1944, subsequently merging with several smaller carriers. Today, as a subsidiary of Alaska Air Group, it has established itself as a dominant air carrier along the west coast of the United States. The airline operates a network of scheduled passenger and cargo routes linking California, Arizona, Idaho, Oregon, Washington and Alaska, Toronto, the former Soviet Union's Far East and four destinations in Mexico – Los Cabos, Mazatlan, Puerto Vallarta and Guadalajara. The airline completed eighteen consecutive profitable years in 1990.

With its headquarters at Tacoma – SEATAC – airport, Seattle, Alaska Airlines has been involved with several mergers, the most recent with Jet America in 1987. On 8 October 1991, Alaska commenced a twice daily round flight with the McDonnell Douglas MD-80 between Los Angeles and Toronto.

The Seattle-based airline became the first customer to order the new extended range MD-83 when it signed for an order for nine airliners during March 1983. The first MD-82 c/n 49232 f/n 1178 N931AS was delivered on 20 February 1985, the second

N930AS c/n 49231 f/n 1177 following on 29 March 1985. Since then the fleet has been steadily added to, and according to the MDC aircraft inventory dated 30 November 1992, Alaska had a fleet of thirty-eight MD-80 airliners, a mixture of MD-82 and MD-83s, with more on order and by 1995 will bring the fleet up to forty plus. On 23 March 1992, the airline took delivery of the thousandth MD-80 produced at Long Beach N960AS c/n 53074 f/n 1976.

As Alaska Airlines MD-80s are withdrawn from service for planned maintenance and overhaul, a new title style is being applied. The airline title 'Alaska' is now styled to take up most of the forward fuselage, and the fuselage cheatline is a single pinstripe now positioned at wing level. The huge indigenous smiling Eskimo motif on the tail unit is retained on a black background rather than the previous blue. Depicted is MD-83 N945AS c/n 49643 f/n 1423 ex G-BNSA of the late British Island Airways (BIA) and procured through the International Lease Finance Corporation on lease. *(MAP)*

ALISARDA (IG/ISS)

Italy

Alisarda was formed on 24 March 1963, with the sole aim of developing tourist services to Costa Smeralda in Sardinia. Today this leading private airline in Italy, but renamed Meridiana, operates an all-jet fleet of six 100-seat Douglas DC-9-51s and five 175-seat McDonnell Douglas MD-82s on both regular scheduled and seasonal services to and from most cities in Italy and including Switzerland, France and Germany. Another eight MD-82 twin-jet airliners are currently on order, delivery to commence during the summer of 1992. It was during 1974 that the airlines first jet services were introduced using Douglas DC-9-14 aircraft. At one time two DC-9-32s were leased and the new MD-82 joined the Alisarda fleet in 1984.

Scheduled services commenced in May 1966, after a period as an air-taxi and charter operator in Sardinia. Today these link Olbia, Milan, Turin, Bologna, Pisa, Rome, Cagliari, Verona, Genoa and Venice. Seasonal services extend as far as Paris, Geneva, Zurich, and Nice. The MD-80 fleet is operated to its full extent during the summer tourist season and were leased out to Overseas National Airways (ONA), at one time the world's largest charter airline, until they ceased operating on 15 September 1978.

The Alisarda livery was attractive with a triple colour cheatline of red and black, divided by a thin yellow pinstripe, this extending nose to tail on an overall white fuselage. The red in the cheatline was centred on the windowline. The title 'ALISARDA' appeared on the fuselage aft of the cockpit. The triple colours mentioned earlier were repeated on the tail unit, with a broad red band taking up one-third of the fin. Engine nacelles were white with 'MD-82' inscribed, and the aircraft registration was white on the red fuselage cheatline and positioned at the rear. Depicted is HB-IKK c/n 49247 f/n 1151 seen on a pre-delivery test flight from the Long Beach factory. It was delivered to Alisarda on 20 September 1984, and today is in service with Meridiana. (MDC)

ALITALIA (AZ/AZA)

Italy

Formed in September 1946, with operations commencing in May 1947, the present name was adopted in 1957, when, with the backing of the present major stockholder, IRI, the two major airlines in Italy, Alitalia and LAI merged. Subsidiary companies include ATI., Aermediterranean, Aeroporti di Roma, and SIGMA. Today Alitalia operates a worldwide network of scheduled passenger services including cargo, from Rome to many points in Europe, Africa, North and South America, the Middle and Far East, and Australia.

Both Alitalia and Linee Aeree Italiane – LAI, with whom the former merged, have a long history of operating Douglas and McDonnell Douglas transport aircraft. The airline over the years has operated the Douglas DC-3, DC-4, DC-6, DC-7, DC-8, DC-9, DC-10 and more recently the MD-82 and the new MD-11 airliner. Today Alitalia and its subsidiary, Aero Transporti Italiani, operate the largest fleet of MD-82s of any airline outside the United States. As of 30 November 1992 the airline has 32 MD-82s in service and

expect by the end of 1996 to have a fleet of no less than 95 of the Long Beach produced airliners. It has been a prolific DC-9 operator since it acquired the first of its DC-9-32s on 8 August, 1967. Three all-cargo DC-9-32Fs were first introduced in May 1968.

The Alitalia colour-scheme is recognised as one of the most attractive. The centre piece of the livery is a stylised 'A' logo in green with a red centre on the tail. The green is a continuation of the windowline and is repeated within the black 'Alitalia' fuselage lettering in black with red again within the 'A'. Small 'Alitalia' titles in gold on the cheatline appear alongside each passenger door. The base colour of the fuselage is white on all airliners in the fleet. Engine cowlings are grey. Depicted is MD-82 carrying dual registration N13627 and I-DAWE c/n 49193 f/n 1127 on a pre-delivery test flight from Long Beach over the Sierra Nevada scenic mountains during 1983. It was delivered on 16 December 1983. (MDC)

ALM – ANTILLEAN AIRLINES (LM/AGP)

Netherland Antilles

Antillaanse Luchtvaart Maatshappij (Antillean Airlines), was formed in 1964 to take over the services of the Caribbean division of KLM, operations commencing during August 1964. On 1 January 1969, ALM's major shareholding was transferred from KLM to the Netherlands Antilles Government. The airline introduced the Douglas DC-9 into service when it acquired three second-hand twin-jet airliners from KLM in the Netherlands, these being later replaced with new or other second-hand airliners. In October 1982, ALM aquired two new MD-82s from McDonnell Douglas, with a third N76823 c/n 49483 f/n 1314 leased from Continental Airlines during April 1988, it remaining basically in Continental livery with ALM tail motif and fuselage title. With the disposal of the earlier DC-9s, the three MD-82s were configured in a two-class seating arrangement with twelve first-class and 126 economy class passengers.

The wide network of ALM operates regional scheduled services from its main base at Curacao to Atlanta, Caracas, Aruba, Benaire,

Georgetown, Granada, Kingston, Miami, Paramaribo, Port of Spain, Port-au-Prince, Santo Domingo, St. Maarten and Valencia. During July 1990, ALM joined the International Air Transport Association – IATA.

Livery of the ALM McDonnell Douglas airliners is colourful and highlighted by two broad fuselage bands of light blue and gold, these sweep from half-way down the fuselage to the tail unit where they narrow. The tail unit carries six gold stars in a circle broken by the title 'ALM' at the base. The title ALM is repeated on the forward fuselage which is off-white to wing level, being light grey lower surface. 'ANTILLEAN AIRWAYS' appears below the windowline on the forward fuselage, whilst 'Super-80' is styled on the engine nacelles. The registration is carried on the fuselage above the engines, and all aircraft carry names. Depicted is MD-82 PJ-SEF c/n 49123 f/n 1075 delivered to ALM on 4 October 1982. *(MAP)*

AMERICAN AIRLINES (AA/AAL)

United States of America

American Airlines today owns the largest airline fleet of any single type in the world – except for the continent once known as the Soviet Union or USSR – currently operating, as of 30 November 1992, no less than 260 MD-82 and MD-83 airliners. Founded in 1934 as a direct successor to American Airways, formed in 1930, and other predecessor companies dating back as far as 1926. Currently operating a fleet of over 450 aircraft consisting of ten types, American is one of the world's largest airlines by any yardstick, and in the past has been instrumental in sponsoring designs which have included the ubiquitous Douglas DC-3, Convair 240 and Convair 990, Lockheed Electra and the Douglas DC-7 and DC-10.

At 30 November 1992, American was operating 59 DC-10s, eleven new MD-11s and 260 MD-80s. The first order for MD-80 airliners, with an initial order for 20, was placed in September 1982, and was the result of a very unique lease arrangement with McDonnell Douglas whereby, the manufacturer agreed to carry not only the cost of training, but also of major maintenance in

return for a low rental. American Airlines agreed to share the profits from its huge 162 Boeing 727 and the MD-80 series fleet. The initial lease was for five years to enable the airline to transfer to an all-new 150 seat airliner if available. High consideration is being given to acquiring the projected MD-90, or possibly configuring new engines for the MD-80 fleet.

Current livery, despite being introduced in 1969, involves a modern look, with a highly polished fuselage and tail unit. This provides an excellent backdrop for a patriotic triple cheatline in red, white and blue, with 'American' title lettering in red, outlined in white, is displayed on the cabin roof. The tail unit hosts dramatically the traditional company motif of a blue eagle swooping down between the peaks of the double 'AA' initials. A small US national flag is carried on the fin. Depicted is MD-82 N288AA c/n 49300 f/n 1219 delivered on 16 August 1985, and seen on a company pre-delivery test flight from Long Beach, and flying over the scenic Sierra mountain terrain. *(MDC)*

ATI – Aero Transporti Italiani (BM/ATI)

Italy

Based in Naples Italy, Aero Transporti Italiani was formed on 13 December 1963, and commenced domestic operations on 3 June 1964. A subsidiary of Alitalia, the national airline of Italy, ATI utilises a large fleet of McDonnell Douglas DC-9-32s and MD-82s with frequent interchanges of aircraft with the parent Alitalia. The airline operates domestic services previously flown by Societa Aerea Mediterranea (SAM). Today operations cover an extensive network of scheduled passenger services linking Turin, Milan, Venice, Verona, Trieste, Udine, Govizia, Genoa, Bologna, Pisa, Florence, Rome, Naples, Bari, Brindisi, Taranto, Lecce, Reggio, Calabria, Messina, Catania, Palermo, Traponi, Siracusa, Marsala, Cagliari, Alghero, Sassari and the islands of Pantellaria and Langedusa.

The McDonnell Douglas aircraft inventory for 30 November 1992, lists 7 DC-9s and 38 MD-80s in service with ATI. However the maximum numbers of each airliner operated in any one year is listed as 26 DC-9-32s and 30 MD-82s, with five of the DC-9s taken over from Aermediterranea when it was merged into ATI during April 1985. The first listed MD-80 for ATI was an MD-82 I-DAWJ c/n 49203 f/n 1174 delivered on 18 December 1984.

Operating Italy's largest domestic route network, the airline also operates group charter flights between Italy, many other European capitals and to North Africa. Major routes served by the successful MDC twin-jet airliners connect Rome with numerous destinations, some already previously listed.

The livery resembles the Alitalia scheme with a stylised 'A' logo in black with a blue centre on the tail. The black is a continuation of the broad windowline and is repeated within the black 'AT' fuselage lettering is black with blue repeated within the 'A'. The base colour of the fuselage is white with grey engine cowling. Depicted is MD-82 I-DAWI c/n 49194 f/n 1130 delivered to Alitalia, the parent airline, on 24 February 1984. The last two letters of the registration is carried on the tail unit, forward of the T-tail. (MDC)

AUSTRAL (AU/AUT)

Argentina

The original Austral airline was formed in 1957, commencing scheduled services in 1958. In 1966 Austral acquired a 30 per cent interest in Aerotransportes Litoral Argentino (ALA) and from that time the companies have operated integrated services. The privately-owned Argentinian airline – Austral Lineas Aereas was established during June 1971 through a merger of Austral Compania Argentina de Transportes Aereos and ALA.

Austral operates a network of scheduled passenger services, radiating on a hub and spoke network from Buenos Aires-Aeroparque. Flagship of the current fleet since it took delivery of its first aircraft on 8 January 1981, is the workhorse McDonnell Douglas MD-80, of which four are in service, and include two MD-81s and two MD-83s. Four more MD-83s were delivered in the autumn of 1992.

The busiest routes of Austral's 155-passenger McDonnell Douglas airliners are a schedule from Buenos Aires to Bahia Blanca, Cordoba, Mar del Plata, Mendoza, Rosario and Tucuman.

Livery for Austral is vivid, displayed on an overall white airliner. An even red/white/blue stripe encompasses the aircraft below the windowline, sweeping up at the tail where it broadens, except for the white, forming the tail unit decor. A break aft of the cockpit gives way for an integrated 'AU' in the same three colours, with the Argentine national flag position lower aft. The title 'AUSTRAL' is positioned forward on top of the fuselage.

The aircraft registration is positioned on the overall white engine nacelles. Depicted is MD-81 N8714Q c/n 48024 f/n 948 delivered on 8 January 1981, and seen on a pre-delivery test flight from Long Beach. Other US registrations quoted for this airliner include N10022 and N13627. All the McDonnell Douglas twin-jet airliners have US civil registrations for some reason. (MDC)

AUSTRIAN AIRLINES (OS/AUA)   Austria

Osterreichische Luftverkehrs – Austrian Airlines – was formed on 30 September 1957, by a merger of Air Austria and Austrian Airways, neither of which, although formed, had commenced operations. The carrier is owned 99 per cent by the Austrian government. Scheduled passenger and cargo services are operated from Vienna, Graz, Linz, Klagenfurt and Salzburg to over 39 cities in nearly as many countries in Eastern and Western Europe and the Middle East.

Austrian Airlines originally placed an order with the Douglas Aircraft Company for nine DC-9-32s for delivery during 1971/72, putting the twin-jet airliners into service on 22 June 1971, with a flight from Vienna to Frankfurt, Germany. All the DC-9-32s, plus five DC-9-51s, the latter introduced into service on 17 September 1975, between Vienna and Munich, have now been phased out. Today the airline fleet consists of nine MD-81s, four MD-82s, one MD-83 and five MD-87s. It was 28 October 1980, when the MD-81

commenced services with Austrian on the Vienna to Zurich sector, whilst the MD-87 opened the Vienna to Zagreb service on 17 December 1987. The order book includes at least a further MD-83 for delivery in 1993. The airline also operates four A310-300 Airbus airliners, but it is the MD-80 fleet which is involved in schedules on the network covering Europe, North Africa and the Middle East.

Austrian Airlines' livery is a simple colour scheme with the tail unit coloured red, white and red, the colours from the Austrian national flag. A white fuselage, with natural metal lower portion, has a red chevron just aft of the cockpit, with the title 'AUSTRIAN' in red behind. The engine nacelles are grey and have a small red chevron near the front. Depicted is MD-81 N1002W c/n 48015 f/n 924 seen on a pre-delivery test flight from Long Beach. It was delivered to Austrian on 16 May 1981 as OE-LDP. *(MDC)*

AVIACO (AO/AYC)   Spain

Aviaco (Aviacion y Commercio) a privately owned airline was formed on 18 February 1948, mainly to operate a network of routes with scope for the generous freight load potential of the new Bristol Type 170 Freighter aircraft. At the time it appeared strange that the Spanish government consented for the formation of Aviaco due to the current political circumstances. During 1950 routes were opened within Spain, to the Balearic Islands and Marseille in France, plus to the Spanish colonies in Africa. A route to Spanish Guinea had to be withdrawn when Iberia also bid for the service, but this loss was compensated for by Aviaco being allowed to open an international service to Brussels and Amsterdam.

By 1960, the Aviaco fleet consisted of a single Douglas DC-6, six twin-engined Convair liners, three Bristol Type 170 Freighters, and four smaller de Havilland aircraft. Currently in 1992 the airline conducts domestic operations in Spain with a fleet of 20 Douglas DC-9s and 13 MD-80s. Four of the latter are flown on lease from

the Guinness Peat Aircraft Group and the International Lease Finance Corporation – two from each.

Deliveries of the McDonnell MD-88 commenced in August 1991, the very first of the model to enter service in Europe, the airline having placed firm orders for thirteen of this successful 155-passenger airliner.

The Aviaco livery consists of a white upper surface, with highly polished lower surface from windowline. An attractive cheatline on the windowline is dark blue and sky blue extending from the cockpit to the rear. The title 'AVIACO' is on the forward top fuselage with styled 'A' which is enlarged and used as the tail unit motif. A small national Spanish flag is forward of the registration on the fuselage over the wing. The engine nacelles are white with 'AYC' imposed, the styled 'A' being incorporated. Depicted is MD-83 EC-EVU delivered as EC-440, c/n 53051 f/n 1718 on 14 June 1990, on lease from the International Lease Finance Corporation. (MAP)

BALAIR AG (BB/BBB/YBB)   Switzerland

The story of Balair goes back to the beginnings of civil aviation in Switzerland. Basically covering two periods, the first being 1925-30, when Balair was an independent airline which then merged with the Zurich based company Ad Astra to form Swissair. The second was the post-war period, when the company was refounded in Basle and became a subsidiary of the present-day Swissair. One could say it is both the parent company and a subsidiary of Swissair.

Over the years Balair has undertaken countless mercy flights during the many international crises and conflicts on behalf of the Swiss government, the United Nations and the International Red Cross organisation. The airline's twenty years of service in the Middle East made it the joint winner of the coveted Nobel Peace prize in 1988.

The Balair fleet is maintained by Swissair and flown by Swissair trained pilots. The cockpit and entire technical equipment conforms to the standards of Swissair and of the KSSU group which consists of KLM, SAS. Swissair and Union de Transports Aeriens (UTA). All aircraft are fitted with fully automatic landing equipment to facilitate landing in the worst visibility.

In Balair service the MD-82 twin-jet airliners, of which three are operated, are fitted out for 149 passengers in a two-class configuration. The single MD-83 seats 147 passengers in a similar seating arrangement. The first Douglas twin-jet joined the airline in November 1976. From 1982 on MD-80s took over mainline, short and medium operations using an MD-81 leased from Swissair. The first Balair aircraft, an MD-82, was delivered on 1 February 1982.

March 1992 saw the introduction of a new dramatic Balair livery consisting of an overall white fuselage with the title 'Balair' in red with yellow dot on the 'i' this taking up most of the forward fuselage. Underneath surface of the airliner from wing level is dark blue. The original red tail unit and white cross are retained. The last three letters of the aircraft registration appear in dark blue on the side of the nose. Depicted is the new livery on HB-INB c/n 49101 f/n 1051 the first MD-80 for Balair. (Balair)

BRITISH ISLAND AIRWAYS (BIA)

United Kingdom

A London-Gatwick based airline, established on 1 April 1982, British Island Airways provided scheduled and charter services with a fleet comprising McDonnell Douglas MD-83s and BAC One-Elevens. Four MD-83 167-seat twin-jet airliners were leased from the International Lease Finance Corporation (ILFC) joining the BIA fleet in December 1987, May and December 1988, and the fourth in April 1989.

In addition to its inclusive tour packages to the usual popular holiday resorts located in Europe and North Africa, British Island Airways operated its popular MD-83s on scheduled passenger services to Catania and Palermo in Sicily, flying from its base at Gatwick, and to Malta in the Mediterranean from both Manchester and Gatwick airports.

Unfortunately the recession, and the general run-down in the United Kingdom tourist traffic, forced the airline out of business on 1 February 1990. British Island Airways suspended all operations on 5 July 1991.

The livery of BIA consisted of a white fuselage and tail unit with a black undersurface. An orange cheatline ran along the windowline, being outlined by a narrow black line. This swept up to the rear of the tail unit and the title 'BIA' was styled on the slope of the cheatline. The title 'British Island Airways' appeared forward on the fuselage below the windowline at wing level. A small Union Jack appeared above the windowline. The registration was in black forward of the engine nacelles which were white. Depicted is MD-83 G-BNSA c/n 49643 f/n 1423 delivered to BIA on the last day of 1987.

BWIA INTERNATIONAL (BW/BWA)

Trinidad & Tobago

Trinidad and Tobago Airways Corporation (BWIA International Airways Corporation) the national carrier of the Caribbean Islands was formed on the first day of 1980, through the merger of British West Indies Airways International and Trinidad and Tobago Air Services (TTAS). The origin dates back to 1940 when the airline was founded as one of the TACA Group of Central American airlines. Control was passed to British South American Airways (BSAA) later merged in British Overseas Airways Corporation (BOAC) in 1947, and the BWIA title was adopted in 1948. In November 1961, the Trinidad Government acquired a 90 per cent holding, followed by the 10 per cent remainder in 1987.

BWIA currently, as of 30 November 1992, has a fleet of one Douglas DC-9-51 and nine McDonnell Douglas MD-83s. The first Douglas twin-jet airliner arrived with BWIA at Port of Spain on 7 May 1986, entering service seven days later on the Port of Spain to Miami sector. It was during the summer of 1976 that BWIA first became a Douglas DC-9 operator when it took delivery of a leased DC-9-51 before acquiring four DC-9-51 airliners of its own, plus a DC-9-34CF. For a short period a single ex Frontier Airlines MD-82 was flown and operated with BWIA between 24 June 1985, and 6 May 1986, on lease from United Airlines.

The colourful BWIA livery was originally introduced in mid 1969, although several small changes have occurred during the last few years. The tail unit carries the popular and striking BWIA emblem – the steel band motif. A gold cheatline commences at the cockpit at windowline level, broadening as it reaches the tail, covering most of the fin and BWIA emblem. The fuselage top is white, as is the forward portion of the fin. The engine nacelles are white and carry the aircraft's registration in black. The underside of the aircraft remains natural metal finish. Along the top of the forward fuselage the airline title 'BWIA' is in red, followed by 'international' in black, then the national flag of Trinidad, with 'Trinidad and Tobago Airways' in black.

The fleet includes one MD-83 9Y-THY c/n 49400 f/n 1356 which was G-PATB with Paramount Airways, no longer operating. Depicted on a pre-delivery test flight from Long Beach is MD-83 9Y-THN c/n 49390 f/n 1269 delivered to BWIA on 25 April 1986. *(MDC)*

CAAC (CA/CCA)

China

The Civil Aviation Administration of China (CAAC), took delivery of the first two of five MD-82 airliners direct from the manufacturer on 12 December 1983. These were for use by its Shanghai and Shenyang Bureaux. The first Shanghai-built MD-82 B2106 c/n 49415 f/n 1260 flew on 2 July 1987. Its FAA certificate was issued four days later, and it was put into service on 4 August from Shenyang by the CAAC. The airliners are now used by both bureaux, renamed in May 1981, China Eastern Airlines and China Northern Airlines. The MD-82 twin-jet airliners serve Hong Kong and Nagasaki, Japan. Following an agreement signed in April 1985, between Shanghai Aviation Industrial Corporation (SAIC), China Aviation Supply Corporation (CASC) and MDC, twenty-five MD-82s were to be assembled in a factory located on the outskirts of Shanghai by SAIC. Major sub-assemblies, avionics, and engines were shipped out by McDonnell Douglas with sub-contractors. The second SAIC assembled MD-82 c/n 49501 f/n 1292 B2107 was delivered on 17 December 1987, and four

airliners were completed in 1988. These included B2108 c/n 49502 f/n 1300; B2109 c/n 49503 f/n 1346; B2120 c/n 49504 f/n 1363 and B2121 c/n 49505 f/n 1381. The production rate was initially on the increase during the first half of 1989, when political turmoil in China plus late deliveries of components from Long Beach slowed down the programme. Shanghai assembled MD-82s joined the five Long Beach built aircraft in service with CAAC.

The livery of Air China is dominated by a large red national flag that appears on the tail with its leading edge parallel to the fin. The white cabin roof and metal lower fuselage are separated by a dark blue windowline, trimmed below by a similarly coloured pin-stripe. 'Air China' titles appear in black Chinese letters on both sides of the fuselage. N1005S is the third Long Beach built MD-82 c/n 49355 f/n 1224 and was photographed on an acceptance flight. It was delivered to Air China on 7 October 1985, registered B2103 *(MDC)*

CANAFRICA-TRANSPORTES AEROS (GC/NCR)

Spain

Canafrica-Transportes Aeros airline was founded in 1985, commencing flight operations during May 1986. In June 1988, after only twenty-five months, the title was changed to AirSur.

Charter flights were undertaken with two McDonnell Douglas MD-83 twin-jet airliners obtained on lease from the huge Guinness Peat Aviation Group in April and May 1987. The 165-passenger jets provided inclusive tours (IT) and services to popular holiday resorts in Portugal, mainland Spain, and the Balearic and Canary Islands from their home base of Madrid. These resorts were served from destinations located in Austria, France, Germany, Italy, Ireland, the United Kingdom, North Africa, West Africa, plus others.

The two McDonnell Douglas MD-83s were EC-ECO c/n 49442 f/n 1358 delivered on 28 April 1987, and EC-ECN c/n 49401 f/n 1357 delivered on 29 April 1987. Both were maintained by Swissair at Kloten airport, Zurich. Depicted is EC-ECN at Zurich.

Livery for the Canafrica-Transportes Aeros MD-83s consisted of an overall white airliner with a dark blue pinstripe under the windowline, this joining a broader dark blue sash aft of the cockpit and disappearing under the aircraft. The tail unit was decorated with a globe motif in blue with a styled 'LA' imposed. The Spanish registration was at the top of the fin. The airline title 'CANAFRICA' was on the fuselage near the front with a small Spanish national flag behind. Engine nacelles were white with 'MD-83' imposed in blue. *(MAP)*

CHINA EASTERN AIRLINES (MU/CEA)

China

In accordance with an agreement signed in April 1985, between Shanghai Aviation Industrial Corporation (SAIC), China Aviation Supply Corporation (CASC), and the McDonnell Douglas Corporation, initially some 25 MD-82s were to be assembled by SAIC in a factory located on the outskirts of Shanghai. The necessary parts, major sub-assemblies, avionics, and engines were shipped to China from Long Beach with the many sub-contractors. The first SAIC assembled MD-82 B-2106 c/n 49415 f/n 1260 made its first flight from Shanghai on 2 July 1987.

The initial operator of the new airliner was the giant General Administration of Civil Aviation of China, known as C.A.A.C. who put B-2106 into regular service on 4 August 1987, A second SAIC assembled MD-82 was delivered in 1987, and four came off the Chinese assembly line during 1988. These joined five Long Beach-assembled aircraft. It was May 1988, when C.A.A.C. was divided into a number of regional airlines. The MD-82s were distributed to China Eastern and China Northern Airlines.

Initially the airline livery of the MD-82s resembled the old C.A.A.C. colours, but both China Eastern and China Northern Airlines have their twin-jet airliners finished in two distinctive colour schemes. China Eastern MD-82s have a white fuselage top and tail unit, this having a divided red and blue circle on which is emblazoned a white Chinese bird-like symbol. On the fuselage from the cockpit aft is the red Chinese national flag, then six red Chinese characters, followed by 'CHINA EAST' also in red. The aircraft registration in red appears just forward of the rear passenger door over the last three windows. Below the window-line three cheatlines in dark orange, light brown and blue encircle the lower fuselage with the orange line enlarging towards the nose. The underside of the fuselage appears to be either natural metal or grey. The engine nacelles are white with 'MD-82' imposed. Depicted in flight is MD-82 B-2107 c/n 49501 f/n 1292 which was delivered on 17 December 1987 from the Shanghai factory. *(MDC)*

CHINA NORTHERN AIRLINES (CJ/CBF)

China

The giant Chinese conglomeration known as the C.A.A.C. – the Civil Aviation Administration of China has now re-organised into a number of regional carriers – since May 1988, using such inspiring titles as China Eastern, Northern, South, Northwest and Southwest Airlines. Initially the national airline of the People's Republic of China operated exclusively with equipment designed and built in the old USSR, with the exception of a number of British-built Hawker Siddeley Trident airliners.

McDonnell Douglas signed an agreement to have their successful MD-82 twin-jet airliner assembled in China.

In December 1983, the C.A.A.C. took delivery of the first two MD-82 airliners direct from Long Beach. The first Shanghai-built MD-82 went into service on 31 July 1987, and so far more than 30 airliners have been assembled in China from components supplied from Long Beach and McDonnell Douglas sub-contractors.

The airline is unusual in that it has adopted a completely new colour scheme. With a white top fuselage and tail unit, the fuselage is decorated with six Chinese characters in dark blue, the airline title 'CHINA NORTHERN' in red, followed by the aircraft registration in dark blue. The white tail unit is decorated with a blue circle which contains a white bird symbol. A broad light blue cheatline envelops the windowline, below it a divided dark blue and red cheatline extended from the cockpit level to the tail. The light blue broadens to envelop the nose. The underside is grey and 'MD-80' appears on the white engine nacelles. Depicted is Long Beach-assembled MD-82 B-2104 c/n 49425 f/n 1240 which was flight tested in California as N1005T. It was delivered to China on 28 November 1985, initially registered with C.A.A.C. and later with China Northern Airlines. *(MAP)*

CONTINENTAL AIRLINES United States of America
(CO/COA)

Owned by the Texas Air Corporation, Continental Airlines is today the fourth largest US carrier, with an extensive network of scheduled passenger services covering 82 domestic and 42 international destinations. Between 1986 and 1987, when it acquired the People Express Group, it had enveloped Frontier Airlines, People Express, Britt Airways and Provincetown & Boston Airlines – PBA. Continental can trace its history back to 15 July 1934, when it commenced services as Varney Speed Lines. Subsequently Varney purchased the Denver to Pueblo route of Wyoming Air Service in May 1937, and moved its headquarters to Denver, Colorado. Later the same year the name Continental Airlines was adopted. It currently has a large mixed fleet which includes 34 Douglas DC-9s and 66 MD-80s as of 30 November 1992. The acquisition of the DC-9s resulted from the take-over of the Texas International fleet in October 1982, and the take-over of New York Air in February 1987. Although Continental

was itself an early DC-9 operator dating back to 4 March 1966, it placed its first order for a single MD-82 in June 1983. Follow-up orders, plus some second-hand aircraft, brought the fleet up to the present mixture of MD-80s, all configured for 24 first class and 117 economy class passengers.

Continental livery has recently changed again, but otherwise has remained basically the same since the original markings were introduced in 1968. The cheatline consists of three basic colours, gold, red and orange. The lower colours have blended giving an appearance of a solid cheatline. 'Continental' in black appears on the cabin roof along with the US national flag and the airline motif in red, this appearing in black on the tail unit. The top of the fuselage and engines are white. Depicted is the first MD-82 for Continental, N803NY c/n 49229 f/n 1140, delivered on 29 June 1984 to New York Air and is still in service. *(MDC)*

CROATIA AIRLINES (CTN)   Croatia/Jugoslavia

Croatia Airlines, a new independent republic in the troubled Jugoslavia after near civil war, commenced operations on 5 May 1991, on the Zagreb to Split route, utilising two McDonnell Douglas MD-82 airliners wet leased from Adria Airways initially until May 1992.

Ljubljana's airport at Brnik was re-opened following the attack upon it by federal Jugoslav forces on 28 June 1991. This was followed by all competancy certificates and insurance cover for Adria Airways being withdrawn, thus enforcing the grounding of its fleet following Slovenia's break-away from the Jugoslav Federation. Adria resumed approximately 40 per cent of its original scheduled flying programme with three Douglas DC-9-30s and two MD-80s. All inclusive tours were cancelled when the civil war in Jugoslavia broke out, however after one month exile from operations into Gatwick, London, the Adria service was resumed.

Slovenia, the new independent republic, adopted the SL-regis-tration prefix for all aircraft operating Adria Airways with effect from noon on 26 December 1991. This was issued by the new Aviation Authority of Slovenia. Included are the two airliners on lease to Croatia Airlines, these being YU-ANC which became registerered SL-ABB c/n 48087 f/n 1035, and YU-ANO which became SL-ABD c/n 49440 f/n 1304.

The Croatia Airlines livery has the simple 'CROATIA AIRLINES' title in thin black on top of the forward fuselage which is white overall. The base of the tail unit is decorated with a light blue triangle at the base with the Jugoslav national flag in the forward corner. A second inverted triangle is chequered red squares. The engine nacelles are white with 'MD-82' imposed, and the registration is on the rear top fuselage. Depicted is MD-82 YU-ANC photographed in 1991 which was delivered to Inex Adria Airways on 2 April 1982. *(MAP)*

CTA (RU/CTA/Z3V)   Switzerland

Compagnie de Transport Aerien (CTA) was formed during September 1978, as a partly owned subsidiary of Swissair to succeed the privately owned charter airline SATA, which closed down operations during the latter half of 1978. CTA operates passenger and cargo charter flights to many points in Europe and the popular Mediterranean holiday area. Operations commenced on 2 November 1978, and after operating successfully with the French designed and built Caravelle airliner, introduced the first of four McDonnell Douglas MD-87 twin-jet airliners into commercial service on 30 April 1988, with a flight to Antalya in Turkey. The 125-passenger airliners are used principally on charter flights from Zurich and Geneva to Greek holiday destinations, the Balearics and Canary Islands, and to Naples and Palermo in Italy. Sub-charters are also flown for the Swissair Group of which it is a member. These sub-charters account for some 40 per cent of the airlines business. The McDonnell Douglas

aircraft inventory dated 30 November 1992, confirms that five MD-87 airliners are still in use by CTA. Early in 1992 it was announced that CTA was to lease two of its MD-87s to Swissair for its Monday to Friday services, and one MD-87 to Balair for the summer season.

The livery for CTA is dominated by the large Swiss national flag emblem on the tail unit. At wing level an attractive cheatline made up of a red/white narrow pinstripe, with a broader red/gold cheatline below encircles the white fuselage. The under surface appears to be dark coloured. The 'CTA' title is styled on the forward fuselage aft of the cockpit. The engine nacelles are white with red pinstripe with 'MD-87' inscribed. The Swiss registration is on the rear of the fuselage under the tail unit in black. Depicted is MD-87 HB/IUC c/n 49587 f/n 1541 delivered to CTA on 16 December 1988, the third of four, and seen at Kloten airport, Zurich. *(MAP)*

DELTA AIR LINES
DL/DAL

United States of America

Founded in 1924 as the world's first commercial crop-dusting company, Delta commenced scheduled passenger services in June 1929, between Dallas, Texas, and Jackson, Mississippi, as Delta Air Service Inc. During the 1930s the airline expanded its services into the states of Alabama, Georgia and South Carolina, and by 1945 the company's routes stretched from Cincinnatti, Ohio, to Chicago, Illinois, from Knoxville, Tennessee, to Charleston, south Carolina and from Savannah, Georgia to Miami, Florida. On its merger with Chicago & Southern Air Lines on 1 May 1953, the airline became known as Delta C & S Air Lines for short. In 1972 it absorbed Northeast Airlines founded in 1933. When this Atlanta based US major airline took over Western Airlines in April 1987, it became the third-largest US carrier.

It took a while for Delta to be impressed with the DC-9 Super 80 when it made its first flight on 18 October 1979, entering service with Pacific Southwest Airlines (PSA) on 17 December 1980. Being one of the few airlines then making a profit, Delta issued a requirement for a new 150-seat aircraft in the Spring of 1981.

Delta's interest was attracted by the MD-80 series which was adaptable to the new technology – the Boeing could not be re-fitted. Delta made a choice and in January 1986, ordered 30 142-seat MD-88s plus 50 options.

The company name Delta is quite unique in that it was originally taken from the Mississippi Delta and is illustrated on all company material by a large dark blue and smaller red delta. This is carried on the tail unit, the fuselage behind the cockpit and on the engine nacelles. This scheme is known as the 'widget.' The tail unit blue delta has the 'DELTA' title in white, this title being repeated on the mainly all-white fuselage, and below the delta on the engine nacelles. Extending along the fuselage is a dark blue cheatline at window level supporting a thin red pinstripe. The blue suitably merges with the anti-dazzle on the nose. Depicted is MD-82, later MD-88, N905DL c/n 49536 f/n 1348 delivered on 28 March 1987, with fleet No.905 in small near the top of the fin. *(MDC)*

FINNAIR (AY/FIN)

Finland

The national airline of Finland has been operating products of the Douglas Aircraft Company since 1941, when it flew the DC-2 airliner. Today it operates the Douglas DC-9-41 and -51, the Douglas DC-10 and the McDonnell Douglas MD-82, -83, and -87, with more MD-82s on order plus the new MD-11. It has a great allegiance to the Long Beach company. Finnair became the launch customer for the MD-83 and MD-87 when it placed orders in February and December 1984 respectively, taking delivery of MD-83 OH-LMR c/n 49284 f/n 1209 on 19 October 1985, and MD-87 OH-LMA c/n 49403 f/n 1404 on 1 November 1987.

The airline was known as Aero until 1968, being originally founded in November 1923, commencing operations in March 1924. Until airports became constructed in 1936, seaplanes were used exclusively. Today Finnair operates one of the world's densest domestic networks, relative to the population, serving a 22-point system. It also operates an extensive network of international scheduled services from its Helsinki base. In all, some 34 destinations are served, mainly in Europe. During October 1989, a co-operative agreement was signed between Finnair, SAS and Swissair and the implementation of practical co-operation commenced on 25 March 1990, with the introduction of summer timetables. Other Finnair partners are Japan Air Systems (JAS) and what was then Aeroflot.

The national flag of Finland and its blue and white colours are the basis of the Finnair livery. An overall white fuselage is divided by a blue cheatline at window level, extending neatly from nose to tail. A light grey cheatline runs parallel with the blue. On the nose is the airline motif, a stylised 'F' for Finnair inset in a blue circle. A rhombus consisting of three shades of blue decorates the lower forward fuselage. The title 'FINNAIR' leaning slightly backwards is on the forward fuselage. A blue cross decorates the tail unit. The engine nacelles are white, and the aircraft registration is on the fuselage in dark blue, forward of the rear passenger door. Depicted is MD-82, marked Super 82 on the engine nacelles, OH-LMN c/n 49150 f/n 1087 seen on a pre-delivery test flight from Long Beach. It was delivered to Finnair on 11 March 1983. *(MDC)*

FRONTIER (FL)

United States of America

Frontier Airlines was formed in June 1950, by a merger of three smaller 1945 formed carriers – Arizona, Monarch and Summit Challenger, and soon evolved into a large US national carrier airline. By the 1960s Frontier was operating in the mid-west from the Canadian border, south as far as Phoenix, Arizona, east as far as Kansas City, and to Salt Lake City westwards. In 1961 some routes were taken over from the large trunk airlines, with Frontier being one of the main beneficiaries. By 1966 the Douglas DC-9 was entering service with many US airlines, however Frontier chose the Boeing 727 which entered service with them on September 30, 1967, these airlines, in the main, loaned by Boeing, pending delivery of the 737. Growth was rapid, and in March 1962, the Goldfield Corporation of San Francisco had purchased Frontier from L.B. Maytag. In a curious switch, Maytag took over National Airlines while Lew Dymond of National, moved to Denver to become president of Frontier. He took over some routes from Continental, and signed a contract to convert the fleet of Convair 340s to Allison prop-turbine power as the 580, these being a great success. By the early 1980s Frontier was operating a large jet fleet of more than 50 airliners including the new

McDonnell Douglas MD-82 twin-jet airliner, taking delivery of the first N9801F c/n 49116 f/n 1061 on 22 April 1982, and operating a further five on lease from Guinness Peat Aviation with effect from 29 April 1986. Four MD-83s were on order when flight operations were suspended on 24 August 1986, and the Denver-based major scheduled airline was acquired by the huge Texas Air Corporation and merged into Continental Airlines two months later.

Utilising a near overall white finish, the Frontier livery was bright consisting of a three-tone fuselage banding of orange/crimson/dark red which enveloped the windowline. This included the nose section, but at mid-fuselage level broadened to envelop the rear upper half of the fuselage. The tail unit was all-white with a red circle on which a stylised 'F' in white was imposed. This 'F' motif was repeated on the top front fuselage, forward of the title 'FRONTIER' in black. The registration was carried on the rear fuselage in red, and the engine nacelles were white. Depicted is MD-82 N9803F c/ 49118 f/n 1065 delivered to Frontier on 13 May 1982, and today this airliner is in service with Continental Airlines, but registered N14889. *(MDC)*

GUINNESS PEAT AVIATION GROUP (AGP)

Eire

The GPA Group, the Irish company built up from nothing over the past fifteen years by Tony Ryan has today become the world's largest aircraft leasing organisation, managing a fleet of nearly 400 aircraft covering a wide variety of modern airliner types. These types include many of the McDonnell Douglas MD-80 twin-jet airliner series. These aircraft have an average age of only 3.7 years and are in service with a large number of airlines around the world. The Guinness Peat Aviation Group makes more than half its profit selling aircraft with operating leases to third party investment.

Irish Aerospace Limited is a joint venture between the GPA Group, the McDonnell Douglas Corporation and Mitsui & Co Limited, involved in operating leases for new McDonnell Douglas MD-83 airliners. Both Irish Aerospace and GPA are located on the outskirts of Shannon airport in County Clare, Ireland. The three letter airline type code for Irish Aerospace is 'IAE'.

Blocks of MD-80 airliners are negotiated with McDonnell Douglas at Long Beach many months in advance for lease to customers in Europe. Often these are allocated temporary Irish registrations, and if the airliner lease is only temporary then this registration is retained. Depicted is MD-82 of Lineas Aereas Canarias registered EI-BWD, it also being operated by British West Indian Airways on a temporary lease. *(MAP)*

HAWAIIAN AIRLINES (HA/HAL)

United States of America

Hawaiian Airlines was founded by the local steamship company as early as 30 January 1929, when it was known as Inter-Island Airways. It opened its services with two Sikorsky S.38 amphibians linking the outer islands of Hawaii with Honolulu on 11 November 1929. Air mail contracts were obtained in 1934 and during the following years the fleet was augmented with the larger Sikorsky S.34 amphibians. A permanent route certificate was awarded by the US Civil Aeronautics Board (CAB) on 16 June 1939, and on 1 October 1941, the airline assumed its present name. In that year three Douglas DC-3s were purchased and on 20 March 1942, an inter-island freight service commenced, which fulfilled a genuine need in transporting perishable foods. Currently Hawaiian Airlines operates scheduled passenger services linking the Hawaiian islands of Lihue, Kauai; Kahului, Maui; Kapulua, West Maui; Hoolehua, Molokai; Lonai; Kona and Hilo, Hawaii.

In the Spring of 1981 Hawaiian Airlines added two McDonnell Douglas MD-81s to its fleet, these being N809HA c/n 48044 f/n 967 delivered on 24 April 1981, and N839HA c/n 48058 f/n 991 delivered on 20 July 1981. The popular twin-jet airliners are utilised on a very high frequency or multiple daily inter-island flights serving seven airports on six islands in the Hawaiian group. The livery of Hawaiian Airlines is attractive with an overall white finish with a red flower and a Hawaiian hula hula girl's portrait imposed which takes up most of the tail unit. A broad double sash envelops the mid-fuselage sweeping to the rear and narrowing. The title 'HAWAIIAN' is on the forward fuselage top with a small flower and maiden's head in front. 'HAWAIIAN AIR' appears on the white engine nacelles and the registration, like all the titles, is in red on the fuselage adjacent to the engines. Depicted is MD-81 N829HA c/n 48051 f/n 975 delivered on 10 June 1981. *(MAP)*

IBERIA (IB)

Spain

Founded in 1940, as Lineas Aereas de Espana, the national airline of Spain came from a succession of air carriers dating back to 1921. The airline is state owned and is controlled through the Instituto Nacional de Industria. During 1990 the airline was being substantially re-organised to create a number of clearly defined profit centres, thus clearing the way for part privatisation. A subsidiary airline, Binter Canarias, was established to operate scheduled passenger services in the Canary Islands, previously provided by Aviaco. Other similar regional airlines are being planned. Iberia is a 48 per cent shareholder in Viva Air, a charter carrier jointly owned with Lufthansa. Today the airline operates a large network of scheduled passenger and cargo services to north, central and south America, Africa, Europe, the Middle and Far East. An extensive domestic network is also provided.

A total of 35 airliners were purchased direct from Douglas, consisting of 31 DC-9-32s and four DC-9-33RCs. All are exten-sively used on Iberia's European network, as well as internal routes, serving major cities in mainland Spain, the Balearics and the Canary Islands. The first Iberia MD-87 EC-290 c/n 49827 f/n 1654 later registered EC-EUF was delivered on 6 April 1990.

The regal livery of Iberia vividly combines the colours of the Spanish flag giving an easy clue to the country's well-known holiday attraction. Triple cheatlines in red, orange and yellow commence aft of the cockpit roof, sweeping along the white fuselage bordering on the windowline. An 'IB' tail motif in red and yellow includes a small gold crown, this representing the return of Spain to a democratic monarchy. The 'IBERIA' title in white is carried on the fuselage on the triple coloured cheatline. Depicted is MD-87 EC-EXR, the registration being duplicated, on the tail and on the fuselage forward of the engines. This was delivered as EC-297 on 20 June 1990, and has c/n 49834 and f/n 1714.

INEX ADRIA AVIOPROMET
(JP/ADR)

Jugoslavia

Known initially as Inex Adria Aviopromet, Inex Adria Airways accepted two Douglas DC-9-32s in April 1969, for its European charter operations out of Brnik airport, Ljubljana for scheduled services to Belgrade the following year. During August 1978, the airline placed an order with McDonnell Douglas for a single MD-81 and two MD-82 twin-jet airliners, these entering service during 1981. Also in service were three DC-9-32/33CF aircraft and the configuration for the MD-81/82 airliners was 167-seats.

Inex Adria introduced jet services which linked Ljubljana, Belgrade, Sarajevo, Skopje, Maribor and Zagreb, whilst external services flew to Munich, Larnaca, Tel Aviv, Athens, Bari, Paris and Gatwick, London. The airliners were also employed on package tour flights and contract charters carrying migrant workers between Jugoslavia and West Germany. On 24 March 1983, Inex Adria Airways commenced its first international scheduled service to Larnaca, followed by Munich, West Germany on 7 December 1984.

Originally formed in 1961, being re-organised in 1968, Adria Airways had its name changed to Inex Adria Aviopromet. In May 1986, the name was changed back to Adria Airways when it became an independent operator.

The tail unit livery for Inex Adria Airways was identical to the current Adria Airways but the fuselage has the windowline boxed in between a dark blue trimline which extends from nose to tail. It is broken by the title 'inex adria airways' forward on top of the white fuselage. Lower surface is light grey. The registration is just forward of the rear passenger door, white on the lower blue cheatline. Depicted is MD-82 YU-ANC c/n 48087 f/n 1035. *(MAP)*

JET AMERICA AIRLINES   United States of America

Jet America Airlines was formed in November 1981, and based at Long Beach airport, California, operating an exclusive fleet of eight locally built McDonnell Douglas MD-82 twin-jet airliners. These were operated on low-cost scheduled passenger services linking California, the mid-west and Texas. Group charters and contract flights were also undertaken. The first two airliners N778JA c/n 48080 f/n 1022 and N779JA c/n 48079 f/n 1016 were delivered from the factory across the street on 13 November 1981, flying the first revenue service between Chicago and Long Beach just three days later on 16 November.

The 147-passenger configured twin-jets, consisting of twelve first-class and 135 coach-class seats, were scheduled on a number of daily flights out of Long Beach, plus other bases at Ontario, Burbank and Oakland, California, serving Chicago,

Dallas/Fort Worth, St. Louis, Las Vegas, Milwaukee and Washington DC. This successful operation of Jet America Airlines continued until the cessation of all operations with MD-82s during November 1987. At least four of the airliners are today operating with Alaska Airlines out of Seattle in Washington state.

Jet America livery was striking with a white fuselage top with the airline title placed forward. A dark blue cheatline envelops the windowline from nose to tail with two red cheatlines below on the white finish which ends at wing level. The tail unit is dark blue with the company motif typifying an aircraft in flight plan view in a dark circle with white outline. The engine nacelles which carry the aircraft registration are light grey. Depicted is MD82 N779JA the second to be delivered. *(MAP)*

KOREAN AIR (KE/KAL)

South Korea

Known until 1984 as Korean Air Lines, Korean Air was formed in June 1962, to succeed Korean National Airlines formed in 1948. Initially wholly owned by the South Korean government, the airline was acquired by the Har Jin Group in 1969. Scheduled passenger and cargo services are operated from Seoul, part of Pusan, and the island of Chegu in South Korea to Tokyo, Osaka, Fukoaka, Nagoya, Niigate, Taipei, Hong Kong, Bangkok, Singapore, Manila, Colombo, Bahrain, Dhahran, Baghdad, Jeddah, Kuwait, Abu Dhabi, Tripoli, Zurich, Frankfurt, London, Amsterdam, Paris, Los Angeles, Honolulu and New York. Korean Air is today one of the world's fastest growing carriers with additional routes now serving Toronto, Vancouver, Rome and Sydney.

First use of the successful McDonnell Douglas twin-jet was when Korean introduced a single DC-9-32 onto its routes in July 1967. By the end of November 1992, this progressive operator had eight of the MD-80 series in service, plus three DC-10s and five MD-11s. Korean was the launch customer for the latter in December 1986.

The impressive new image of Korean Air was unveiled early in 1984, when it replaced the previous red, white and blue Korean Air Lines scheme which dated back to the 1960s. The airline decided to not only change the livery design, but also to adopt a completely new company motif, and adopt a more dynamic title. The current livery consists of a pale shade of blue which covers the entire upper fuselage half, this representing the sky, whilst below the blue runs a silver cheatline with the underside in pale grey. The engine nacelles are blue. The company logo, known as the 'Taeguk' combines the red and blue of heaven and earth. White has been added to represent the 'never ending strength of progress'. This appears on the tail unit. It also forms the letter 'O' within the dark blue title 'Korean Air.' fuselage titles. The South Korean national flag appears at the top of the fin towards the trailing edge. Depicted is MD-82 HL7273 c/n 49374 f/n 1208 delivered on 21 August 1985, and seen over the Sierras on a pre-delivery test flight from Long Beach *(MDC)*

LINEAS AEREAS CANARIAS (EN/9L/LCN)

Spain

Lineas Aereas Canarias (LAC), is based in Tenerife in the Canary islands, and operates charter passenger and cargo services from its base at Tenerife airport to Europe and North Africa. The small airline was formed during 1985, and today operates a fleet of five McDonnell Douglas MD-83 twin-jet airliners. Operations commenced on 25 September 1985, utilising a single Vickers Viscount prop-jet which operated between Tenerife and Lanzarote. The first MD-83 was delivered to LAC on 19 October 1987, this being joined later by four more, all on lease from the Guinness Peat Aviation Group. In addition to inter-island services Lineas Aereas Canarias operates on passenger and cargo charters to the holiday resorts in the Canarias from various points in Germany, Italy, France, the United Kingdom, Scandinavia, Morocco and Gambia. The airline livery for LAC consists of an overall white airliner with two fuselage red stripes which commence thin and low at the nose, broadening out to the wing where they split and finish with a sweep up to the lower tail portion. The tail unit is decorated with a red disc representing the sunshine and the title 'LAC' in black is at the top of the fin. The airline title is on the fuselage top with 'LINEAS AEREAS' small and 'CANARIAS' large. The engine nacelles are white. Depicted is an unidentified MD-83 of LAC. *(MAP)*

LAV (LV/LAV)

Venezuela

Abbreviated as LAV, Linea Aeropostal Venezolana was founded in 1930. The French Aeropostale company which had commenced services in Venezuela in 1929, never achieved its ambition of linking France and the Caribbean via Natal, French Guiana and Venezuela. At the same time as the formation of Air France and the subsequent dissolution of Aeropostale, the Venezuelan branch of the airline was bought by the Venezuelan government, which renamed it LAV. At first this company formed part of the Ministry of Labour and Communications, but in 1937 it became an autonomous government-owned corporation. By 1938 its French designed and built Latecoere 28s were replaced by Lockheed Electras and Lodestars. New capital was provided and the route network was extended. The next year the headquarters were transferred from Maracay to Maiquetia, the airport for Caracas, and the fleet was further modernized by the acquisition of ubiquitous Douglas DC-3 airliners.

This government-controlled airline took delivery of its first Douglas DC-9, a DC-9-14, on 23 October 1968, and today operates an all McDonnell Douglas twin-jet airliner fleet consisting of one DC-9-15, three DC-9-32s, one DC-9-34CF, eight DC-9-51s plus six MD-83s, the first of the latter acquired in 1986. With the wide variety of different size models LAV can provide a wide variety of seating capabilities ranging from 85 in the small DC-9-15, to 163 passengers in the MD-83.

The LAV livery consists of a white fuselage top, grey lower half, with an attractive dark blue cheatline with light blue pinstripe below, this extending down the fuselage below the windowline. The tail unit is divided into three sections which are dark blue/white/dark blue. A gold bird motif is imposed on the centre white section, this bird motif being repeated on the fuselage top aft of the cockpit next to the title 'AEROPOSTAL' in dark blue followed by the Venezuelan national flag. The engine nacelles are white and the airliner registration is carried on the rear fuselage top, adjacent to the engines. Depicted is MD-83 YV-36C c/n 49395 f/n 1286 delivered to LAV on 30 June 1986, and seen over scenic Sierra Nevada mountains during a pre-delivery test flight from Long Beach. *(MDC)*

MARTINAIR (MP/MPH/YMP) The Netherlands

The Martinair company was formed in May 1958, initially named Martin's Air Charter, the present title being adopted in 1974. It operated as an aerial advertising company and giving joy rides, using a Douglas DC-3 transport. By the spring of 1988, the company commenced scheduled transatlantic passenger services from its base at Amsterdam, serving Baltimore, Boston, Chicago, Cleveland, Detroit, Los Angeles, Miami, Minneapolis, New York (JFK), San Francisco and Seattle in the United States and Toronto in Canada. However the major part of the company's business is the operation of passenger and cargo charters worldwide. Share-holders include the Royal Nedlloyd Group, KLM., and a number of various financial institutions. Associate companies are very active in the field of flight training, sales support by hostess teams, party catering and the production of deep freeze meals and com-ponents. In Amsterdam the Mart Inn restaurant is operated.

Martinair has been a Douglas DC-9 operator since 1 August 1968, when it introduced the type on its European and Mediterranean routes. These were three RC (rapid change) airliners. The fleet was joined later by another DC-9 and three leased MD-82s, the latter being introduced during 1981. The current three MD-82s, of which the first was PH-MCD c/n 48022 f/n 1079 delivered on 28 March 1983, are fitted out for 165 passengers, or in cargo configuration can carry up to 12.5 tons of freight.

The airline's colour scheme includes a deep red windowline which on the smaller aircraft type doubles back to form a stylised red 'M' tail logo. Black 'Martinair Holland' fuselage titles boldly announce the company name. The fuselage top and side, plus engines, are white, the under fuselage remaining natural metal. Depicted is the second MD-82 for Martinair, PH-MBZ c/n 49144 f/n 1096 delivered on 15 February 1983, and seen on a pre-acceptance test flight from Long Beach. As of 31 October 1991, it was still in service, and PH-MCD had been disposed of. *(MDC)*

MERIDIANA SPA (IG/ISS/ZJ7)   Italy

Meridiana is a new airline that has emerged from nearly three decades of experience. An outgrowth of Alisarda, Universair, Lineas Aereas Canarias, and the general aviation company, Euravia, it has one of the youngest aircraft fleet of all major southern European carriers and is based at Olbia, Sardinia. Twenty-nine years ago, in March 1963, it was launched as Alisarda with two eight-seater Beechcraft C-45 aircraft operating on an air taxi and charter service. By 1992 it had become the largest privately owned airline in Italy with a fleet of six Douglas DC-9-51s, eight McDonnell Douglas MD-82s and three BAe 146-200s, with more MD-82s on order for delivery in early 1992.

   The year 1983 was historic as the airline decided to buy two of the latest 172-seat MD-82s these being Swiss registered – HB-IKK c/n 49247 f/n 1151 delivered on 20 September 1984, and HB-IKL c/n 49261 f/n 1153 delivered seven days later. A third MD-82 was purchased in 1986, I-SMET c/n 49531 f/n 1362 delivered 21 May 1987. Between the end of 1989 and April 1990 Alisarda took delivery of three 130-seat DC-9-51 twin-jet airliners. In 1990 the airline carried 1,547,290 passengers.

   On 1 September 1991 the name changed to Meridiana which is derived from the meridional cultures of Southern Europe and the Earth's meridian. From its southern hubs, the airline is positioned to expand its services to destinations of all points north, south, east and west. London, Gatwick, Munich and Paris (Charles de Gaulle) are linked daily with Florence, whilst Barcelona, Frankfurt and Zurich are linked with Florence five days of the week. Meridiana pilots are trained in the simulators of Swissair and SAS airlines.

   With the change of name Meridiana exploited the opportunity to change its look and livery. Red, yellow and purple cheatline runs the full length of an overall white fuselage. The tail unit has an upper red portion on which is the new logo, a styled white globe. This logo precedes the title 'Meridiana' on the front fuselage top, whilst the registration plus a small Italian national flag are positioned at the rear of the fuselage. Engine nacelles are white with 'MD-82' inscribed. Depicted is I-SMER in flight over typical southern Italy terrain c/n 49901 f/n 1766. *(Meridiana)*

MIDWAY AIRLINES (ML/MID)

United States of America

Midway Airlines was formed in 1976, commencing operations on 1 November 1979, utilising a small fleet of three 63-seat twin-jet Douglas DC-9-14s acquired from Trans World Airlines, the routes including a link with Midway airport, Chicago, with Cleveland, Detroit and Kansas City. By the end of the first year of operations the number of Douglas DC-9s in the fleet had increased to seven. The airline acquired Air Florida during 1984, its route services operated for a period as Midway Express. The commuter carrier Fischer Bros. Aviation was acquired in May 1987, this operating as Midway Commuter. By March 1990 Midway was providing scheduled passenger services to no less than 54 destinations from hubs at its home base, Midway, Chicago, and Philadelphia. The latter hub was opened on 15 November 1989, with flights serving Sarasota, Tampa, West Palm Beach, Albany, Buffalo, Boston and Hartford-Springfield. Midway Commuter, mentioned earlier, operated to 25 destinations, together with Iowa Airways, both operating under the Midway Connection banner.

Midway operated four models of the successful MD-80 series,

these being the 120-seat MD-87, the MD-88, MD-83 and MD-82, the latter three models seating 143 passengers, and all fitted with eight first class seats. On 29 March 1989, when the first MD-87 – N801ML c/n 49724 f/n 1549 – was delivered, Midway Airlines announced a massive $900 million order for 37 MD-80s with a further 37 on option. These were scheduled to be delivered between 1993 and 1997. The airline was able to boast one of the highest daily utilisation of any DC-9/MD-80 operator in service, quoting 11 hours.

The Midway livery constituted a white fuselage with a red underside, the slightly staggered title 'Midway' in red on the forward fuselage. The tail unit is in red except for a white band on the leading edge with a stylised 'M' in white angled on the red portion of the tail. A dark cheatline surrounds the fuselage at wing level and this sweeps up the tail unit in unison with the white. The US registration is on the white engine nacelles. Depicted is MD-87 N803ML c/n 49726 f/n 1610 delivered on 19 July 1989, and seen during the last few months of the airline's operation in 1991.

MINERVE S.A. (FQ/MIN/Z9U)   France

Minerve (Compagnie Francaise de Transports Aeriens) was formed in June 1975 and is a privately owned airline, founded by Rene F. Meyer. Both passenger and cargo charter operations commenced in November 1975, to various points in Europe, the Middle East, Africa, the Far East and the Americas. By March 1985 the Minerve fleet had increased to include a Douglas DC-8-73, a Douglas DC-8-62CF, a Douglas DC-8-53, one French designed and built SE 210 Caravelle 6N and a Piper Aztec. The McDonnell Douglas MD-83 twin-jet airliner was first introduced into service in April 1987, with F-GGMA c/n 49399 f/n 1343 being delivered on 18 March 1987, in order to further develop its medium haul operations throughout Europe. Configured for 169 passengers, the MD-83s in the fleet fly charters from Paris and other French cities to a wide variety of European destinations, the holiday resorts on the Mediterranean, and even venture as far as West Africa and the Middle East.

McDonnell Douglas MD-83s operated by the airline have also been utilised by Minerve (Canada) on operations in North America.

The Long Beach built airliners are leased from both the Guinness Peat Aviation Group and Irish Aerospace. Looking ahead Minerve has options on at least two more MD-83s for delivery in October and November 1994, with plans to eventually add a further six MD-83s to the fleet. During peak holiday business periods the airline has found it necessary to lease MD-83s from other operators, mainly Air Liberte, an example being MD-83 F-GHEB c/n 49822 f/n 1539 leased during 1991. With the introduction of the MD-83 airliners in 1987 it was decided that a new corporate image was required, this featuring the head of the Roman goddess Minerva, after whom the airline is named, and appearing in a red disc on the tail unit. Fuselage stripes of burgundy, white, blue and red are below the windowline from nose to tail. The airline title 'Minerve' is on the forward fuselage top and the French tri-colour flag is positioned to the rear of the fuselage above the windowline. 'SUPER 83' is inscribed on the white engine nacelles. Depicted is MD-83 F-GGMB c/n 49617 f/n 1464. *(Chris Doggett)*

MUSE AIR CORPORATION United States of America

Muse Air was formed in 1981 by Lamar Muse, former president of Southwest Airlines, to operate high-frequency scheduled passenger services, commencing with the route from Love Field, Dallas, to Hobby airport, Houston, this being inaugurated on 15 July 1981. Eventually the airline services were extended to serve nine cities in five states in the west and south-west United States. Over the years, the airline built up its fleet to include six 155-seat twin-jet McDonnell Douglas MD-82s, two similar MD-83s and ten 130-seat Douglas DC-9-51s. These served the extended network which included services to Oklahoma City, Los Angeles, San Diego, New Orleans, Orlando, Miami and Tampa in Florida. It also added the Texas communities of Brownsville, McAllen, San Antonio, Lubbock and Midland/Odessa. A single Douglas DC-9-33RC was leased from the manufacturer at Long Beach.

On 30 June 1985, the stock of Muse Air was purchased by Southwest Airlines, who renamed the company Transtar Airlines on 17 February 1986. As a result of substantial operating losses it was decided on 1 July 1987, to discontinue operations, and all scheduled flights ceased in August. All aircraft were sold including delivery positions for two more McDonnell Douglas MD-82 twin-jet airliners.

The Muse Air livery was simple, but quite unusual and yet attractive with an overall white fuselage with the title 'Muse Air' written in a large long-hand type style on the forward fuselage. This was repeated, smaller, on the tail unit. The airliner registration was carried on the fuselage below the rear passenger door. (MDC)

NEW YORK AIR (NY/NYA) United States of America

New York Air was a publicly-held national carrier with a controlling interest held by the huge Texas Air Corporation. The carrier began scheduled passenger services on 19 December 1980, and served Boston, Washington DC., New Orleans, Detroit, Tampa/St. Petersburg, Orlando and Raleigh/Durham from its two bases located at New York's La Guardia and Newark airports. High-frequency non-stop jet services in direct competition with Eastern Air Lines 'Air Shuttle', linked La Guardia with Washington National Airport, and Boston. Both were also served from Newark airport, located in New Jersey. In addition the route network also took in points in Ohio, Georgia, Florida, Louisiana, Tennessee plus North and South Carolina. During February 1987, New York Air was integrated into Continental Airlines, also a subsidiary of the Texas Air Corporation.

A striking rich red fuselage down to wing level, identified the New York Air livery on the airline's Boeing 737-300s, the 16 Douglas DC-9-31/32 110 seat twin-jet airliners, and the 14 McDonnell Douglas MD-82s with 147 seats, the latter introduced in September 1982. The DC-9s were involved on low-fare scheduled services. The red livery had a red pinstripe border. A heart-shaped motif decorated the tail unit, also red, outlined in white. The title 'NEW YORK AIR' was in white on the mid fuselage top, the engine nacelles were also red with the registration in white.

Depicted is MD-82 N807NY c/n 49261 c/n 1153 delivered to New York Air on 5 September 1984. Today this airliner is in service in Continental colours, but registered N16807. (MDC)

NORTHWEST AIRLINES (NORTHWEST ORIENT AIRLINES) (NW/NWA)

United States of America

Founded on 1 August 1926 as Northwest Airways, this airline adopted the title Northwest Orient Airlines in 1934. The company was re-organised in 1985 to form NWA Inc. a holding company for Northwest Airlines and several other subsidiaries. The carrier merged with Republic Airlines in 1986. The airline was the launch customer for the Boeing 747-400 introducing the type on its trans Pacific routes in June 1989. The MDC aircraft inventory for 30 November 1992 lists 149 DC-9, eight MD-80, and 29 DC-10 airliners.

Northwest Airlines inherited a large fleet of McDonnell Douglas twin-jets from its merger with Republic Airlines on 12 August 1986. These included 29 DC-9-14, five DC-9-15RCs, 61 DC–31/32s, 28 DC-9-51s and eight MD-80s. A further 16 DC-9-30s were purchased later, together with 12 DC-9-41s. The airline operates the MDC twin-jets into a number of mid-sized markets from its three domestic hubs in the United States.

A broad battleship grey fuselage band is the main feature of the new livery assumed in early 1992, this being just above wing level. The top of the fuselage and the tail unit are scarlet red. The airline motif is in white on the fin and the title 'NORTHWEST' in broad letters in white on the grey forward on the fuselage. Under surface is white and a small national flag is painted forward. Engine nacelles are grey and registration white on the grey. Depicted is MD-82 N314RC c/n 49110 f/n 1062 delivered to Republic Airlines on 26 August 1983 as N1004L. *(Chris Doggett)*

NORWAY AIRLINES (JA)   Norway

Norway Airlines, formerly known as Air Europe Scandinavia, is a scheduled and charter passenger airline. It was formed in 1987 initially operating as a passenger charter carrier utilising a single Boeing 737. It was taken over by the International Leisure Group, to become Air Europe Scandinavia. It was purchased from the liquidator of Airlines of Europe, parent of Air Europe, the United Kingdom based operator which ceased trading in 1991. Today Sterling Airways has a 30.7 per cent interest, others being Fokus Invest AS with 43.2 per cent and Lyng Industries AS with 11.9 per cent.

The airline serves Oslo to London (Gatwick) Airport and has made application to operate from Bergen and Stavanger to Gatwick. Plans to operate inter-Scandinavian single-class low-fare services, using leased McDonnell Douglas MD-80 twin-jet airliners, is already in operation.

With over one hundred and twenty employees, Norway Airlines, in addition to operating two Boeing 737-300 airliners, has leased a single MD-87 SE-DHG c/n 49389 f/n 1333. All are based at the airline's headquarters at Oslo airport. The MD-87 is leased from Transwede (Aeroswede) who are based at Stockholm – Arlando, Sweden.

Livery for Norway Airlines consists of an overall white airliner with an all red tail unit on which is imposed a styled segmented wheel in white. Three neat cheatlines decorate the lower fuselage below the windowline these being red, black and dark blue. The airline title, 'NORWAY' in black, 'AIRLINES' in red, is styled on the forward fuselage top whilst the aircraft registration plus the Norwegian national flag appear on the fuselage just forward of the all-white engine nacelles on which is inscribed 'MD-87'. Depicted is MD-87 SE-DHG which was originally registered to the Douglas Aircraft Company at Long Beach, California, as N287MD on 13 January 1987, and delivered to Transwede Airways as SE-DHG on 8 April 1988. (MAP)

OASIS INTERNATIONAL AIRLINES (AAN/YGA)

Spain

Oasis International Airlines, formerly known as Andalusair, is a Spanish charter carrier, operating passenger charter flights to European and Canary Island holiday resort destinations. Oasis commenced operation with the McDonnell Douglas MD-83 twin-jet airliner on 27 May 1988, flying a Malaga to Manchester return service. The airliners are configured for 165 passengers, and it operates an extensive charter network linking Madrid, Malaga and the Balearic Islands and the Canary Islands with pick-up points in the United Kingdom, northern Italy, Germany, France and other European countries.

The McDonnell Douglas aircraft inventory for 30 November 1992, lists Oasis as having a fleet of six MD-83 airliners, three of these being held on lease from the Guinness Peat Aviation Group based in Shannon, Eire. Oasis is based at Palma airport, Majorca.

Quite a number of MD-83s have been listed with Oasis livery, this now being standardised as illustrated. The airliners are white overall with an emerald green tail unit which has the airline's attractive white motif. The title 'OASIS' is carried on the lower forward fuselage. The registration is carried above the windowline forward of the white engine nacelles, with a small Spanish national flag in front of the registration. The emerald green of the tail unit sweeps down to include the rear of the fuselage. Depicted is MD-83 EC-FEB c/n 49619 f/n 1483. *(Chris Doggett)*

PSA PACIFIC SOUTHWEST AIRLINES (PS)
United States of America

Pacific Southwest Airlines, once one of the US leading inter-state carriers with an annual passenger total of nearly four million, had a history which read like an early Hollywood movie script. With determination, and a sense of humour, the management of a once very profitable San Diego flight training school decided to form an airline. In May 1949 PSA commenced operations with a single leased Douglas DC-3, making once-a-week flights between San Diego and Oakland, near San Francisco. According to all the rules of business and common sense, the new airline should not have been successful. It had no support from tax subsidies or air mail revenues. Yet, nearly 20 years later PSA was operating over 900 flights a week up and down the Californian coastline and constantly expanded its service.

The airline grew very rapidly, and in August 1978 placed an order with Long Beach for ten new MD-81s, taking delivery of the first N924PS c/n 48034 f/n 946 on 14 November 1980. The fleet continued to grow and eventually numbered 20 MD-81s and 11 MD-82s, both configured for 150 passengers. Five more on order

were cancelled. At its peak the airline's MD-80 jet fleet accounted for almost 300 daily departures, serving a galaxy of destinations in the Western States of California, Arizona, Nevada, New Mexico, Oregon and Washington. The routes were served until 9 April 1988, when the airline was absorbed by US Air.

The PSA livery was simple with a white finish to the upper half of the airliner with the title 'PSA' in red forward of the fuselage behind the cockpit and on the lower tail unit. A thin red cheatline went round the aircraft below the cabin and cockpit at window level, whilst a second red cheatline commenced behind the cockpit above the cabin windows broadening as it reached the tail unit then sweeping up the aft of the fin. The registration was in red at the rear of the fuselage between the two cheatlines. Pacific Southwest Airlines appeared in small letters in red, below the cabin window below 'PSA'. Lower half of the airliner plus wings remained in natural finish. Depicted is Douglas DC-9-81 N982PS c/n 48052 f/n 974 delivered to PSA on 15 May 1981. *(MDC)*

PARAMOUNT AIRWAYS (QJ/PAT)

United Kingdom

Paramount Airways commenced operations from Bristol Airport on 1 May 1987, and was the first British airline to operate the successful McDonnell Douglas MD-80 Series twin-jet airliner. It operated a total of four MD-83 airliners on lease from the Irish Guinness Peat Aviation Group. The 165-seat aircraft were employed on inclusive tour (IT) flights from Belfast, Cardiff, Exeter and from its home base at Bristol, to major holiday resorts in Europe, the Mediterranean and to the Canary Islands.

The first MD-83 was delivered on 24 April 1987, and the fourth just over a year later, on 29 April 1988. It was during August 1989 that Paramount suffered problems and was put under administration pending receivership. A rescue package failed because the airline was unable to secure sufficient winter flight contracts

and the four aircraft were repossessed by the lessor, Guinness Peat. Paramount ceased operations on 2 November 1989, and entered receivership.

The Paramount livery consisted of an overall white fuselage with a red/white/blue narrow cheatline which extended down the fuselage below the windowline. At the front this expanded into a broad sash sweeping downwards, and at the tail the cheatline swept up the tail, to expand once more across the fin. The title 'PARAMOUNT' was styled on the forward top fuselage, with small company motif forward, and Union Jack aft. The engine nacelles were white and had 'MD-83' imposed, whilst the registration was positioned at the rear of the airliner. Depicted is G-PATB c/n 49400 f/n 1356 delivered to Paramount on 24 July 1987.

REPUBLIC AIRLINES   United States of America

Formed in June 1979 by a merger of North Central Airlines of Minneapolis-St. Paul and Southern Airways of Atlanta, Georgia, Republic commenced operations on 1 July 1979, and on 1 October 1985, acquired Hughes Air West, thus strengthening its position as a major US carrier. The combined network of scheduled passenger and cargo services linked more than 100 cities in no less than 32 states of the continental USA. The routes flown also covered the District of Columbia, Canada, Mexico, and Grand Cayman in the Caribbean. The airline became public-owned with 42,000 stockholders. The largest fleet of Douglas DC-9s in the world, at the time, came from the combined fleets from North Central and Southern, as well as from Hughes Air West. On 12 August 1986, Republic merged with Northwest Airlines with a transfer of all the Republic fleet including the MD-82s.

The Republic livery on the MD-82 consisted of a white top and a blue grey lower surface. A light blue double cheatline extended from below the cockpit to the rear of the fuselage, encasing the windowline, and having a dark blue thin stripe border. The title 'REPUBLIC' was contained in a break in the upper cheatline, aft of the cockpit. The trailing edge of the tail unit was in light blue. An airline relic of the North Central days, 'Herman' the mallard duck insignia created in 1947, was prominent in light blue on the tail unit. The engine nacelles were blue grey with a small US national flag imposed. Depicted is MD-82 N307RC c/n 48086 f/n 1029 delivered to Republic on 21 December 1981, and transferred to Northwest on 12 August 1986, it is still in service today. *(EMCS)*

SAS – SCANDINAVIAN AIRLINES SYSTEM (SK/SAS)

Denmark, Norway, Sweden

The national flag carrier of Denmark, Norway and Sweden has been a profitable operator of airline products produced by the Douglas Aircraft Company and McDonnell Douglas for many years, having operated most of the Douglas Commercial types produced. It is unique in having a DC-9 Series built specifically to its own requirements, this being the DC-9-41 which was introduced into service in May 1968, on its short-haul intra-Scandinavian network.

Formed in 1946, the owners of SAS are Det Danske Luftfartselskoep A/S (Danish Airlines), Det Norske Luftfartselskoep A/S (Norwegian Airlines) and AB Aerotransport (Swedish Airlines). Since formation SAS has operated scheduled transatlantic services, and all routes of the three airlines are now operated by SAS. An extensive network of Scandinavian and European scheduled passenger and cargo services is operated, together with routes to Africa. The McDonnell Douglas aircraft inventory dated 31 March 1992 reveals that SAS operates 41 Douglas DC-9s and 62 McDonnell Douglas MD-80s. More of the latter type are on order plus options. The first of the MD-80 series was an MD-81 OY-KGT

c/n 49380 f/n 1225 delivered on 10 October 1985. Subsequently 133-seat MD-81s, 156-seat single-class MD-82s, 133-seat MD-83s, and 110-seat MD-97s are all in service. The DC-9s and MD-80s are used extensively on main European routes and extensively within the Scandinavian countries. On 24 November 1991, an MD-82 SE-DPH c/n 49663 f/n 1437 for Scanair, ex EC-EUF, was put into service between Stockholm and Stansted. It had accumulated 7,837 hours and had 5,215 landings.

In 1983 board approval was given to the current colourful SAS livery, in preference to two similar designs submitted, and this is worn by the large fleet. A white fuselage overall, it has a striking rhombus in the three national colours of the participating nations, Denmark, Norway, Sweden in that sequence. Simple 'SCANDINAVIAN' title is on the fuselage in dark blue outlined in gold. This colour applies to the 'SAS' on the tail unit. The three national flags appear on the engine nacelles, and the aircraft registration is on the fuselage forward of the rear passenger door. Depicted in landing sequence is MD-81 SE-DFR c/n 49422 f/n 1264 ex SE-DFV and delivered to SAS on 26 March 1986. *(MAP)*

SCANAIR (SK/DK/YPA)   Scandinavia

Formed on 30 June 1961, as a Danish charter company. On 1 October 1965, the company was reorganised as a Scandinavia charter consortium owned by ABA (Swedish Airlines), DDL (Danish Airlines) and DNL (Norwegian Airlines) in a 3.2.2. proportion. Scanair, the charter subsidy of the huge Scandinavian Airlines system (SAS), operates contract charter and inclusive-tour flights from Stockholm, Goteborg, Malmo, Oslo and Copenhagen to some fifteen or more destinations in winter. These are chiefly centred on the Canary Islands. In summer Scanair serves popular holiday resorts in the Mediterranean, Miami, Barbados and the Bahamas. It operates to Germany, Austria, France, the United Kingdom and Switzerland, whilst charters as far afield as Gambia have been undertaken. The airline has operated a variety of types over the years including, in addition to the Douglas DC-10, the Douglas DC-8, the Boeing 747 and A300 Airbus. In addition it leases aircraft from both SAS and Lingeflyg,

including the MD-80 twin-jet airliner. The photograph above illustrating Scanair livery is of MD-83 LN-RMB c/n 49557 f/n 1436 ex LN-RLV delivered on 11 February 1988, to SAS.

Unveiled in 1983, shortly after the new image introduced by the Scandinavian Airlines System (SAS), the Scanair livery reflects the close links with the parent company. A pure white fuselage finish displays six sunshine coloured stripes, five broad and one narrow below dark blue 'Scanair' titles. These are aft of the cockpit. The national flags of Denmark, Norway and Sweden appear neatly side by side on the rear fuselage, always in that sequence. The all-white tail-unit displays a huge orange sun. On the MD-80 series of airliners the words 'Sun Jet' appear on the white engine nacelles in sunshine orange. Depicted is LN-RMB an MD-83, c/n 49567 f/n 1436.

As of 30 November 1992 Scanair operated four MD-83 twin-jet airliners.

SPANAIR (NR/SPP/Z9R)   Spain

Spanair commenced operations during March 1988, flying passenger charter services to destinations in Europe and the Canary Islands. The company is jointly owned by SAS Leisure and Viajes Morsano, a Spanish travel retailer and tour operator. The airline is based in Palma, Majorca, and the fleet of McDonnell Douglas twin-jet airliners were obtained on lease from both Irish Aerospace and the Guinness Peat Aviation Group. All the popular Spanish holiday destinations are served, as well as destinations in the United Kingdom, Norway, Sweden, Denmark, Germany, France and the Benelux countries, Switzerland, Austria, Italy and Greece.

The first revenue flight for Spanair took place on 1 June 1988, from its home base at Palma de Mallorca (Majorca) to Bilbao. As of 30 November 1992, the McDonnell Douglas aircraft inventory disclosed that the Spanair fleet consisted of nine MD-83s, these being configured in an all-tourist configuration for 163-passengers.

The livery for Spanair is bright and simple with a large 'Spanair' title situated on the forward fuselage which is overall white. The registration, plus a small Spanish national flag appears under the windowline by the wing. The tail unit carries a very attractive red and blue wave design, this being repeated small on the white engine nacelles. Depicted is MD-83 EC-EIG c/n 49579 f/n 1465 delivered to Spanair on 25 April 1988. *(MAP)*

SWISSAIR (SR/SWR)   Switzerland

Swissair was formed on 26 March 1931, when Ad Astra Aero and Basle Air Transport (Balair) became amalgamated; becoming Swiss Air Transport Company – Swissair. Ad Astra was founded in 1919, and commenced flying-boat operations in Switzerland prior to pioneering international routes. The route network initially covered just 2,800 miles, and at the end of 1931, Swissair's staff totalled 64. In April 1932, the airline became the first European carrier to operate US built aircraft. Two years later the airline introduced the twin-engined 16-seat Curtiss Condor, and became the first European carrier to employ stewardesses. In 1935, Swissair operated the 14-seat Douglas DC-2 airliner with which it established a link between Zurich and London via Basle.

The Swiss national carrier became the launch customer, along with Austrian Airlines, for the MD-80 Series when it ordered 15 with five options in October 1977. The first MD-81 HB-INC c/n 48002 f/n 938 was delivered to the airline on 13 September 1980, and the first MD-81 service took place on 5 October 1980, flying a Zurich to Frankfurt round trip. A total of 24 114-seat, three-class MD-81s are currently in service. The airline is scheduled to lease two additional airliners from Guinness Peat Aviation in the Spring of 1993, which will raise the MD-81 fleet to 26.

The livery of Swissair is very distinctive with the Swiss national flag occupying the complete tail unit. This is complemented by bright red 'Swissair' titles on a white fuselage top. Two cheatlines, the upper in brown, lower in black, extend from nose to tail below the windowline level. The lower fuslage is finished in light grey. Depicted is MD-81 c/n 48002 f/n 938 the first one for Swissair registered N1002G and seen on a pre-delivery test flight prior to delivery on 13 September 1980. It became HB-INC. *(MDC)*

TDA-TOA DOMESTIC AIRLINES (JD/TDA)

Japan

The airline was founded on 15 May 1971, by the merger of Japan Domestic Airlines and Toa Airways. Since April 1988, TDA has been operating as Japan Air System. The airline operates an extensive scheduled domestic network, involving no less than 66 trunk and regional routes serving 38 cities. Charter services are also provided throughout southern Asia. Shareholders include Tokyo Corporation, Japan Air Lines, Toa Kosan and Kinki Nippon Railway.

Orders have been placed with Long Beach on a regular basis which will eventually bring the total to 32 MD-80 airliners with deliveries due up to 1997. The progressive build-up of the MD-81 fleet has meant the release of the DC-9-41s, these being sold to Airborne Express in the USA. Apart from the 128-seat DC-9-41s and the 163-seat MD-81s, the current inventory includes four 130-seat MD-87s introduced in 1988, these providing multiple daily non-stop services to most major points on the main Japanese islands and Okinawa far south, all operating from its primary traffic hubs located at Tokyo, Osaka, Sapporo, Fukuoka and Kagoshima. The airline has placed an order for ten of the new projected McDonnell Douglas MD-90-31 airliners.

The TDA livery is very attractive, consisting of a white top fuselage with a very broad cheatline below windowline level, this made up of four colours – yellow, orange, red and dark blue in descending order. These commence at the nose and continue to the rear of the fuselage, with a broad dark blue predominant fin stripe with the fuselage colour of yellow at the rear of the tail unit. The 'TDA' title is in white on the dark blue fin stripe. The upper white fuselage has dark blue titling in both English and Japanese, the lower fuselage on the MD-81 being a natural metal finish. Depicted is MD-81 JA8497 c/n 49281 f/n 1200 delivered to TDA on 20 May 1985, and still in service. *(AP Photo Library)*

TRADEWINDS (MI/SQA)   Singapore

Tradewinds Charters (Tradewinds Private) was formed on 17 February 1975, as a charter subsidiary of Singapore Airlines to operate passenger and cargo charter flights, using Singapore aircraft and crews as necessary. It was based at Changi airport, Singapore.

In January 1989 a single new McDonnell Douglas MD-87 twin-jet airliner was acquired from the Guinness Peat Aviation Group on a two-year lease with an option to renew the contract for a further two years. The 130-seat MD-87 9V-TRY c/n 49673 f/n 1508 operated on scheduled regional services from Singapore to Kuantan, Malaysia; to Hat Yai, Phuket and Pattaya in Thailand; and to Kaohsiung in Taiwan. However, as anticipated, the lease of the MD-87 was not renewed. The MDC airliner was leased by

Guinness Peat to Mexico initially with TAESA in 1991 and more recently LATUR and registered XA-RUO.

It is interesting to record that the MD-87 c/n 49673 f/n 1508 was registered to the Douglas Aircraft Company on 7 September 1988, prior to going to Guinness Peat for lease to Tradewinds.

The livery included an overall white fuselage with the title 'Tradewinds' on the forward fuselage above the windowline with a national flag of Singapore aft of the title. The tail unit was turquoise blue with a white bird with outstretched wings imposed. The rear of the fuselage was emerald green and the registration was on the fuselage above the windowline forward of the white engine nacelles. Depicted is MD-87 9V-TRY in Tradewinds livery during 1991. *(Chris Doggett)*

TRANSTAR

United States of America

On 30 June 1985, the stock of Muse Air was purchased by Southwest Airlines, who renamed the company TranStar Airlines on 17 February 1986. As a result of substantial operating losses it was decided on 1 July 1987, to discontinue operations, with all scheduled flights ceasing during August. All the airliners were sold, including delivery positions for two more McDonnell Douglas MD-82 twin-jet airliners. Muse Air had built up its fleet to include six 158-seat MD-82s and two similar capacity MD-83s plus ten 130-seat Douglas DC-9-51s. During its very short life, TranStar served an extended route network which included Oklahoma City, Los Angeles, San Diego, New Orleans, Orlando, Miami, Tampa, and the Texan communities of Brownsville, McAllen, San Antonio, Lubbock and Midland/Odessa.

McDonnell Douglas MD-82 N936MC c/n 49444 f/n 1323 and MD-82 N937MC c/n 49450 f/n 1324 were both delivered to TranStar on 12 December 1986, the latter operating today with Continental Airlines still registered N937MC.

The TranStar livery consists of an overall dark blue aircraft with the title 'TranStar' in sky blue below the windowline on the forward fuselage. The registration is sky blue and placed on the rear of the fuselage aft of the wing. Five narrow, wavy, pinstripes circle the rear fuselage, the colour sequence being pink/green/blue/pink and green, the latter pinstripe running up the tail unit. Depicted is MD-81 N935MC c/n 49125 f/n 1074 which is unusual in having all-white engine nacelles. *(MAP)*

TRANSWEDE (GM/TWE/Z6K)　　　Sweden

Transwede Airways AB, a Swedish passenger carrier was formed on 1 April 1985, to operate inclusive-low IT charters from Sweden and Norway with a Sud-Aviation Caravelle 10B. The company is owned by NRT Nordisk AB. During July 1987, the airline placed an order with McDonnell Douglas for two MD-87 twin-jet airliners, the first of which, SE-DHG c/n 49389 f/n 1333, was delivered on 4 August 1988. Four MD-83s had already been acquired by Transwede on lease. The 161-seat MD-83s and 132-seat MD-87s are used extensively on holiday flights to popular resorts in the Mediterranean, the Canaries, Israel and to and from airports in the United Kingdom. The airline's daily utilisation is one of the highest achieved by an MD-80 operator, being in excess of ten hours.

In the autumn of 1991 Norway Airlines of Oslo, Transwede of Stockholm and Sterling of Copenhagen, formed an alliance called the Transnordic Group, aimed at reducing Scandinavian air fares by as much as thirty per cent. Both Norway Airlines and Transwede have commenced scheduled services to London Gatwick and achieved considerable success with their one-class service. The air group is hoping to cash in on the impending liberalisation of European air routes.

Largely generated through its sister tour operators, Transwede has rapidly expanded from carrying 70,000 passengers in 1986, to 960,000 in 1990. Initially the airline operated four different types of aircraft in an eleven strong fleet. Today it operates six MD-83s and two MD-87s and by 1995 the fleet will be increased to ten as more MD-83s are scheduled for delivery in 1994 and 1995. The response to the one class service has been excellent from both business and leisure travellers alike.

The livery of Transwede consists of an overall white airliner, with a distinctive broad three colour band in dark blue, light blue and yellow which adorns the front fuselage, and also acts as a tail unit band. The same colours are used for fuselage bands which extend along the fuselage under the level of the windowline, sweeping upwards to join the tail bands. The title 'TRANSWEDE' is in dark blue on the fuselage behind the cockpit, while the registration is positioned above the last three passenger windows. Engine nacelles are white with 'MD-83' inscribed. Depicted in flight is MD-83 SE-DHB c/n 49396 f/n 1305 delivered to Transwede on 24 September 1986. (MDC)

TWA – TRANS WORLD AIRLINES (TW/TWA)

United States of America

Trans World Airlines (TWA) was founded on 13 July 1925, as Western Air Express which had merged with Transcontinental Air Transport. Both airlines had extended their networks by buying up other companies. TAT bought Maddux Airlines late in 1929, whilst early in 1930 WAE bought Standard Air Lines. From the beginning TWA was in the forefront of airline service. The title was changed to Trans World Airlines on 17 May 1950.

During October 1982, TWA negotiated favourable lease terms from McDonnell Douglas, similar to those obtained by American Airlines, for 15 MD-82s. The fleet has since grown with the first MD-82 being delivered on 18 April 1983, – N901TW c/n 49166 f/n 1098. The 142 passenger airline seating 12-first class and 130 economy class seats fly the airlines domestic network serving the Atlantic and Pacific seaboards and Florida.

The colour scheme of TWA was officially unveiled on 30 November 1974, it replacing the traditional 'twin-globe' scheme. The 'Trans World' titling appears in solid red; replacing the previous red outline. Two red cheatlines commence at the nose, under the black anti-dazzle panels, proceeding along the white fuselage below the windowline. The cheatlines then widen as they continue and ultimately meet at the rear of the fuselage. The 'TWA' logo in white appears on the tail unit, proud on a red section which covers most of the tail. This livery description applies to the TWA MD-82 airliner. Some types carry the US national flag either at the top of the fin or on the fuselage by the registration. The fleet number appears on the nose. The McDonnell Douglas twin-jet airliners are rapidly accumulating high flying hours and being retired. Depicted is the second TWA MD-82 delivered, N902TW c/n 49153 f/n 1101 delivered on 27 April 1983, with fleet No.9002 and seen on a pre-delivery test flight from Long Beach. (MDC)

TUR AVRUPA AIRLINES (IAE/TUR/ZQE)

Turkey

This company, also quoted as TUR European Airways, commenced operations in May 1988, originally as a joint venture between the Kavala Group and TEA of Belgium originally operating a TEA Boeing 737-200. TUR operates inclusive tour flights to West Germany, Scandinavia and the United Kingdom, customers including the German tour operator Neckermann. Home base for the airline is Antalya, Turkey. As of March 1990, TUR was operating two Boeing 727-200 and two Boeing 727-100 airliners.

The McDonnell Douglas aircraft inventory for 30 November 1992 lists two MD-80 twin-jet airliners. This includes MD-83 TC-TRU c/n 49442 f/n 1358 obtained from one of the Irish lease

companies ex EI-CBO. The MD-80 archives reveal that it was originally delivered as EC-ECO to Canafrica on 28 April 1987.

The livery of TUR Avrupa Airlines is simple and includes an impressive stylised 'TUR' on the fuselage, this repeated somewhat smaller on the tail unit. A small Turkish national flag is positioned on the fuselage forward of the title which is in blue. The main part of the fuselage is white finish, with dark blue underside, this blue sweeping up the rear side of the tail. Two blue and one red narrow cheatlines surround the fuselage at just above wing level, these sweeping up onto the tail in front of the broad blue stripe. The registration TC-TRU is carried on the engine nacelles. *(MAP)*

UNIFLY EXPRESS (IP/IPP)   Italy

Unifly Express was founded in 1980 and is a privately owned carrier, with its main airline fleet consisting of two leased McDonnell Douglas MD-83s, two MD-82s, plus two Douglas DC-9-15Fs, the latter acquired in March and May 1988, when the airline commenced DC-9 operations. A Fokker F.28 airliner is also used by Unifly Express.

The airliners are used on ad hoc and contract passenger and freight operations out of Ciampino airport at Rome, to European and Mediterranean holiday resorts and as far as the Canary Islands.

Two more MD-83s were delivered in May 1991, in addition to three MD-83s which arrived in Rome in February and March 1991. The twin-jets were due to be transferred to the airline's Milan based subsidiary, Alinard Spa, for its scheduled domestic and regional services. Alinard Spa, an Italian regional airline operates scheduled passenger services from Taranto to Milan via Perugia and Taranto to Bergamo via Rome. This airline was sold to Unifly Express in January 1990, but continues to operate as a separate company, concentrating on scheduled services with Unifly's DC-9 and MD-83 airliners, with the possibility of using a new hub at Palermo. Charter flights are also undertaken.

Unifly Express has a brilliant red finish to its airliners extending down as far as wing level and including the tail unit and engine nacelles. A blue pinstripe is supplemented by a broader gold stripe this encircling the airliner. The tail unit has a gold circle with a white aircraft type motif plus other decorations. The airline title 'Unifly Express' is in gold on the forward fuselage. The two cheatlines mentioned earlier also decorate the engine nacelles. Depicted is MD-82 EI-BTY c/n 49667 f/n 1466 leased from the Guinness Peat Aviation Group and delivered to Unifly Express on 15 May 1988. *(MAP)*

US AIR (US/USA)   United States of America

US Air, originally known as All American Aviation, was founded on 5 March 1937, to pioneer a highly specialised mail service. This incorporated the use of devices for dropping and picking up mail in flight and by this means fifty-eight small communities in Pennsylvania, Delaware, Maryland, West Virginia and Ohio received a regular air mail service from September 1938 until June 1949, when the service ended. By this time the airline had become a normal certificated local carrier. All American Aviation adopted the title Allegheny Airlines during 1953, and the present name, US Air, dates from October 1979. During 1968, Lake Central Airlines was acquired, and in 1972 Mohawk Airlines, with both Pacific Southwest Airlines and Piedmont Airlines following in 1987.

US Air completed the integration of Piedmont Airlines on 5 August 1989, creating an airline with over 420 jet aircraft and more than 48,500 employees. Today, and several acquisitions later, US Air is one of the world's largest airlines, serving almost 200 points in 36 states in the United States and overseas. It was Allegheny who

placed the Douglas DC-9 in service on 1 September 1966, with a, single DC-9-14 airliner. Today, according to the McDonnell Douglas aircraft inventory for 30 November 1992, the fleet consists of 73 Douglas DC-9s and 31 McDonnell Douglas MD-80s. This fleet is made up of 19 MD-81s and 12 MD-82s obtained through the April 1988 acquisition of Pacific Southwest Airlines, and in September 1992 these were joined by 20 new MD-82s orderd during early 1989.

The US Air livery consists of a polished natural metal finish, with a three colour – crimson/red/black-fuselage stripe just above wing level which is sectioned with black at the rear. The triple coloured band sweeps up the rear of the tail unit. The airline title is in two colours 'US' red and 'AIR' black on the forward fuselage. The engine nacelles are black and the aircraft registration is on the fuselage adjacent to the engines. Depicted is MD-81 N802US c/n 48036 f/n 963 ex N926PS of Pacific Southwest Airlines to whom it was delivered on 9 March 1981. *(MAP)*

VIASA (VA/VIA)   Venezuela

VIASA was formed in 1961 to take over the international routes operated by AVENSA and LAV, which now concentrate on domestic routes in Venezuela. The international flag carrier of Venezuela operates scheduled passenger and cargo services from Caracas, Maracaibo, Porlamar and Barcelona across the Atlantic to Lisbon, Orporto, Santiago de Compostela, Madrid, Zurich, Paris, Milan, Rome, London, Frankfurt and Amsterdam.

During 1989 the airline commenced a Caracus to Havana service and added Sao Paulo to the Caracas to Rio route. Charter flights are operated to Toronto and Vancouver during the winter season. The airline is wholly owed by the Venezuelan government.

Early in 1991 the VIASA fleet consisted of two A300 B4 Airbus five Douglas DC-10s and one DC-8-61HF. Since then the fleet has been increased to three Airbus and six DC-10s, with the DC-8 being disposed of. For a very short time in 1983/4 two MD-82s were utilised on the VIASA network to South America and the Caribbean. The two twin-jet airliners – YV158C c/n 49103 f/n 1083 and YV159C c/n 49104 f/n 1085 – were both delivered on 30 December 1982. Unfortunately severe financial difficulties caused the cancellation of many services and a reduction in the airline fleet, this resulting in the disposal of both MD-82s to Jet America Airlines on 30 May 1984.

The colour scheme of VIASA includes a dark orange tail unit with white 'VIASA' letters. The upper fuselage is white with dark orange 'VIASA' lettering behind the cockpit and blue 'VENEZUELA' over the wings on the fuselage. A blue cheat line envelops the windowline and the lower fuselage is natural metal with grey engine nacelles. Depicted is MD-82 N1005B c/n 49103 f/n 1083 with US temporary registration on a pre-delivery test flight from Long Beach. It was delivered to VIASA as YV158C on 30 December 1982. *(MDC)*

ZAS – AIRLINE OF EGYPT (ZA/ZAS)   Egypt

Zarkani Aviation Services (ZAS) known as Airline of Egypt was formed in June 1982, and was granted a commercial passenger carrying licence during September 1987. A single McDonnell Douglas MD-82 twin-jet airliner was acquired in March 1988 on lease from the manufacturer in Long Beach, this being supplemented by a 115-seat Douglas DC-9-33CF also obtained on lease.

The total airline fleet consists of three Boeing 707s, two Lockheed Jetstars, five MD-83s, with at least a further MD-83 on order. The five MD-83s are fitted out for 167 passengers carried in a single-class layout, and in addition to the domestic routes are utilised on the airlines scheduled Cairo to Amsterdam route. The MDC airliners are also employed on inclusive tour (IT) charters.

ZAS operates a domestic network of scheduled services between its Cairo base and Alexandria, Aswan, Hurghada, Luxor and Sharm El Sheik. It was announced in March 1991 that the Boeing 707s and Lockheed Jetstars were up for sale.

The airline livery for ZAS is attractive, the airliner being in an overall white finish with a blue fuselage cheatline on the windowline and a dark blue pinstripe below this, both tapering and joining at the nose. The title 'AIRLINE OF EGYPT' is dark blue on the top of the fuselage with 'Zas' in red and the title in Arabic towards the rear. The tail unit has a styled 'Z' in blue with an inscription in Arabic below. The engine nacelles are white and with N848CP, later SU-DAM, depicted, the registration is on the nacelles it having c/n 49848 f/n 1592. *(MAP)*